WATCHING OUT

Julian Burnside, QC, is an Australian barrister who specialises in commercial litigation and is also deeply involved in human-rights work, in particular in relation to refugees. He is a former president of Liberty Victoria, and is also passionately involved in the arts: he is the chair of Melbourne arts venue fortyfivedownstairs, and regularly commissions music. He has published a children's book, *Matilda and the Dragon*, as well as *Wordwatching*, a collection of essays on the uses and abuses of the English language, and *Watching Brief: reflections on human rights, law, and justice*.

Julian Burnside

Watching Out

reflections on justice and injustice

SCRIBE
Melbourne • London

Scribe Publications
18–20 Edward St, Brunswick, Victoria 3056, Australia
2 John St, Clerkenwell, London, WC1N 2ES, United Kingdom

Published by Scribe 2017

Typeset in 12/15.75 pt Granjon by the publishers
Printed and bound in Australia by Griffin Press

 The paper this book is printed on is certified against the Forest
Stewardship Council® Standards. Griffin Press holds FSC
chain of custody certification SGS-COC-005088. FSC promotes
environmentally responsible, socially beneficial, and economically
viable management of the world's forests.

Scribe Publications is committed to the sustainable use of natural resources
and the use of paper products made responsibly from those resources.

9781925322323 (Australian edition)
9781925548501 (e-book)

A CiP entry for this title is available from the National Library of Australia

scribepublications.com.au
scribepublications.co.uk

To Kate:
Without her support, I could not have kept going.

Contents

Introduction

This book does not set out to equip the lay reader to mount his or her own litigation. Neither is it designed to help law students pass their exams or to teach lawyers how to practise law; rather, I hope it will remind some lawyers *why* we practise law.

Although I try to explain some of the basics of the law and of legal procedure, I do so only to make the rest of the book intelligible. The real purpose of this book is to explore the reasons we have a legal system at all, to look at the way it operates in practice, and to point out some ways in which its operation does (or does not) run true to its ultimate purposes.

WHEN I FIRST contemplated the project of writing this book, I was uncertain what it was to be about. It was not to be an autobiography, or a collection of war stories. It was not to be a legal textbook. I thought perhaps it was to be a book about the justice system.

I told a friend about it. With her solid pragmatism, she pointed out that we do not have a justice system: we have a legal system. But a book about the legal system sounds to me a bit too much like a textbook. And, anyway, I am not sure how much the legal system interests me. I wanted to write about the way our system of justice works. Justice interests me much more than law does. So this is a book about a chimera: a creature that does not exist, but that is real enough in the mind.

Everyone has an instinct for justice. We develop it early. As Tom Stoppard says in *Professional Foul*, even children in the playground understand justice: their cry 'It's not fair' recognises a truth 'which precedes utterance'. A powerful concern about justice, or indignation at injustice, is a very common trait. It is tempting to say it is universal, but experience makes that difficult to defend. Everyone who is concerned about justice and injustice is likely to have their own, idiosyncratic reasons for it. I have written before a few fragmentary observations about its origins in my own life. But I have not told the whole truth.

As I have written before, in *Watching Brief*, an experience at school was part of it:

> On my last day at school, when the glittering prizes were being strewn among the chosen, I was awarded colours in each of my sports. But I was awarded only second colours, because they were only second-colour sports. I still remember the stinging injustice of it, that for a good footballer the ultimate accolade of first colours for playing a season for the school; yet after representing the school at the highest level for years as a swimmer, and in diving and rugby, I got second best.
>
> If I were to speculate on the origin of my concern about justice I would settle for that day.

That was part of it, but not all of it. As a rather insecure child in a family that was falling apart, decades before such things were normal or socially acceptable, I found life very confusing and uncertain. Above all other things, I needed to understand how life worked, so that I could feel safer. I understood that there were rules about how you were to behave: rules made by government (I knew these were called 'laws'), rules made by school, requirements imposed at home as house rules. Although house rules were the lowest in the pecking order, they seemed the most important. As a small child, I made sure to keep my room tidy, to help with the washing up, and so on. In short, I was scrupulous at home to adhere to all the rules and requirements in the hope that this would bring happiness. Looking back on it, I must have been an insufferable little goody-goody.

By contrast, my brother was a tear-away. Younger than me by two years, he completely disregarded the rules and did what he wanted. By the time he was eight years old, he broke rules more often than he adhered to them. It got him into a lot of trouble, but he had the advantage of a sunny, charming disposition, which I conspicuously lacked.

When he was about 10 years old, he became ill. He was admitted to hospital, and spent the summer of 1962 recovering. He had acute appendicitis, we were told, and sported an impressive scar in consequence.

After his appendicitis, he continued in his rule-breaking ways, but got away with it. What troubled me — and confused me — was that he was never punished for his transgressions. Initially, I suppose I put it down to the obvious principle that you don't punish sick children, and he was sick for quite a long time. And by the time he was better, the fact that he was not punished for breaking the rules had simply become an ingrained habit of the family. But I began to resent it, increasingly. I pressed on, being a conspicuous goody-goody, while Ian did what he pleased. This reached a low point, in my thinking at least, with 'The Cutty Sark incident'.

Several years earlier, I had built a scale model of the great 19th-century wool clipper, the Cutty Sark. It took hundreds of hours to make, and I remember that the rigging took about 40 yards of string. It was a truly magificent thing that would not have been possible, but for my youthful obsessiveness. I came home one day and found that Ian had used it in a mock sea battle in the compost heap, and had burnt it to the waterline. I was apoplectic. Even now, nearly a lifetime later, the image of it pains me. He was not disciplined for it. The impression I had was that my anger was somehow inappropriate.

More than a decade later, I learnt the truth of it. When he was 20, Ian visited Geelong and could not be bothered waiting for a train back to Melbourne, so he broke yet another rule: he hitched a ride. The driver was incompetent, and ran off the road on a bend. The car ended up in a creek. Ian hit his head on the door pillar, and, unconscious, drowned in the creek. The driver walked away unhurt. (Later, at the inquest, his counsel criticised Ian for hitch-hiking. This stung bitterly, and to me, as a fifth-year law student, it left its own distinct mark,).After Ian's death, and in the emotional havoc it caused in what remained of our family, my sister and I learned the truth about Ian's 'appendicitis'. In fact, he had been diagnosed with a rare form of cancer, of which only eight cases were then known: four had survived to puberty. My mother had favoured him because she had every reason to think that he was living under a death sentence. I wish she had told us before this: my sense of injustice about his being favoured would have disappeared.

At that time, especially, and since then, I have had reason to reflect on the nature of justice and injustice. My mother's active discrimination in favour of my brother was a kind of justice to him and, had I understood it, would not have been an injustice to me. The way she went about it was wrong (as I saw it), but understandable. Any criticism of the justice system has to take account of the fact that the concept of justice is subtle and complex, and may depend on the position of the observer.

When put to the test, most people have difficulty identifying what justice is, especially when there is tension between proper process and a desired result. Due process is inherent in our conception of justice. But bad process can yield the right result, just as good process can produce the wrong result. The legal system is designed to produce justice. We call it the justice system — sometimes un-self-consciously, sometimes with bitter irony. It is designed to produce justice according to law. Whether it achieves that goal is not the subject of general agreement.

Although I spent much of my childhood shadowed by a sense of injustice at the way things were, I had no plans to become a lawyer. In fact, I had no clear idea what I wanted to be once school was over. I knew I did not want to follow my father into a career in medicine. That was probably a disappointment to him. He was a very skilled and successful urologist; he had established the urology clinic at Melbourne's Alfred Hospital. On occasions, during my early teens, he took me with him to watch him operate. I would gown and scrub up, and stand by the operating table watching the operation proceed: an abstract of red and yellow, framed by pale-green sheets. I marvelled at the skill with which he could make an abdominal incision, locate the relevant bits, and then sew up the wound, tying the knots with one hand.

I can recall very precisely the moment when I decided that this was not the job for me. He was operating on a patient who had a stone in a ureter, which was blocking the flow of urine from one kidney to the bladder. I watched as he cut through the skin and sub-cutaneous fat to expose the abdominal muscle. He stabbed his scalpel through the first layer, then put his index fingers into the cut and tore the muscle apart with a sound like tearing a blanket. The point of this was that muscle fibres were separated from each other but not cut. He repeated this process with the other two layers of abdominal muscle. Having found his way into the workspace, he located the ureter and the small bulge where the stone was. Then he invited me to feel it. So far, this had all been an interesting intellectual abstraction: a pattern of green, yellow, and red. But the warm, slippery feel of the patient's guts suddenly pitched the experience onto a different and unwelcome plane. The theatre sister obviously noticed my face drain of enthusiasm, and led me to a chair. After that, a career in surgery was off the agenda.

MY UNCERTAINTY ABOUT career choices did not worry me. I have always been a late developer. Having plodded through school with no great distinction and no particular plans, year 12 (Matriculation, as we knew it then) was pretty good to me. I won four prizes and two scholarships, as well as second colours for rugby and swimming (bitterly). I was offered places in several faculties at both Melbourne University and the recently established Monash University. A person I knew and liked was studying law at Monash, so I chose to enrol in law there. My theory was that, in the terrors of a new and unfamiliar environment, it would be nice to know someone. As it happened, I hardly ever saw my friend there.

Studying law was quite good fun, but I was not inspired by a burning desire to make a career of it. I entertained vague ideas of being an artist. Why that idea took hold remains a mystery to me: I was always attracted to the arts, especially painting and photography, but even with the vanity of youth I did not reckon my skills sufficient to make it a paying proposition. While I spent hundreds of hours taking, developing, and printing black-and-white photographs during my university years, the only photographs that made me any money were of weddings, babies, and amateur car races. These were, between them, a handy source of income for a student, but hardly the stuff of a career as an artist.

In my second year of law, for obscure reasons, I also enrolled in the Faculty of Economics and Politics. As I had conceived the tentative possibility of becoming a management consultant, I majored in accounting and economics. For the next few years, my thinking was increasingly fixed on the prospect of joining a firm such as Coopers & Lybrand (as they then were). It is hard to imagine now, but in the late 1960s there was real doubt about whether any law firm would hire law graduates from Monash. These were the years when the Vietnam war was an increasing source of social and political division. Chief stirrer at Monash University was the shambling, brilliant, quixotic

Albert Langer. Langer, and others at Monash, urged the student body to take part in the Moratorium marches, arranged by the charismatic Jim Cairns. Monash was seen as a hot-bed of radical political activism. This, it was said, would effectively prevent Monash law students from being employable in the legal profession. In hindsight, this was an unduly pessimistic assessment.

I was not much troubled by these ideas, because I was not intending to be a lawyer. I took part in the Moratorium marches, and in the later demonstrations at Olympic Park against the tour of the Springboks rugby team from South Africa, but I did so as staff photographer for *Lot's Wife*, the Monash student newspaper. To my shame, I had not formed any views about the issues that gave rise to those great political protests.

As I have written elsewhere, I had no interest in politics at all, and had not bothered to form views about political issues. My family, fragmented though it was by divorce and other squabbles, was staunchly united in supporting the conservative side of politics. As a result, I voted Liberal as a matter of habit, rather than from any sense of conviction. The best I can say of this, looking back on it, is that I was at least true to my indifference. By the time I was 18, I had a powerful reason for opposing Harold Holt's Coalition government and the war in Vietnam: my birthday had come up in the ballot that determined who was to be conscripted into the army. I was entitled to defer my call-up until I finished my university course. I did this, and was due to be called up at the start of 1973.

Conscription (especially conscription, which chose some but not others) was an unpopular and divisive measure. It fell to be tested at the federal election in December 1972, in which I voted Liberal. Gough Whitlam won and, as he had promised, his Labor government immediately abolished conscription. My vote in the 1972 election might, by some, be regarded as a principled and altruistic thing, but it was just political indifference and naïvete. I mention these things because, very much later, I was publicly critical of the conservative government led by John Howard. Many people tried publicly to explain this as having been caused by my lifelong adherence to Labor politics. Their comments were irritating to me, and grossly erroneous, but also amusing in view of the fact that I had voted Liberal in every election from 1972 (when I was first eligible to vote) to 1996, including the highly charged election in 1975 after the dismissal of the Whitlam government. Having voted for John Howard in 1996, I was dismayed to learn what the Coalition government had been up to in connection with waterfront reform. Their conduct culminated in the bitter dispute between the Maritime Union of Australia and Patrick Stevedores in 1998.

Not long before the monumental election of December 1972, an accidental turn of events disrupted what might laughingly be called my 'career plans'. In those unenlightened times, mooting was mostly a voluntary activity at Monash. A moot is a kind of mock court, in which law students play the role of barristers arguing an appeal case. As mooting was mostly voluntary, it was mostly the domain of nerds. I mooted whenever I got the chance. So it happened that I was invited to join the Monash intervarsity mooting team to compete in the Australia and New Zealand Law Students Society mooting competition in Auckland in 1971. At that time, I had never even been to Tasmania. The idea of being flown to New Zealand was very exciting.

Monash did quite well. We got into the final moot, but came second. As luck would have it, I was awarded the Blackstone Cup as best individual mooter. (There's a title to conjure with.) The prize-giving ceremony was sufficiently noteworthy that the Auckland newspaper had a paragraph about it the next day. At this illustrious function, I was introduced to Sir Richard Wild, the chief justice of New Zealand, who had presided over the final moot. He asked me what I planned to do. I said I was thinking of being a management consultant. He told me, 'You should go to the bar.'

This was the most important person I had ever met, so it seemed a good idea to follow his advice. I had only the vaguest idea of what life at the bar involved, but I decided that I would be a barrister.

It occurred to me recently how entertaining it would be if what he had meant was, 'Go and get another glass of wine'. I quite like the idea of having built my life on a misunderstanding.

One of my friends on the Monash team was Bill Wallace — one of the gentlest and cleverest people I have ever met. At Christmas that year he presented me with Irving Stone's biography of Clarence Darrow. That book was one of the strongest formative influences in my budding career.

Darrow was a remarkable American advocate. He was a campaigner for causes. He once said, 'As long as the world shall last there will be wrongs, and if no man objected and no man rebelled, those wrongs would last forever.' He did himself and his family and his practice great harm by embracing causes that were deeply unfashionable and dangerously unpopular.

Darrow was a champion of the labour movement, a vocal opponent of prohibition, a prominent humanitarian, and a tireless campaigner against the death penalty. It is not easy to bring to mind now just how dangerous it was in America a century ago to support the labour unions: they were suspected of being anarchists and socialists. It is easy to forget that embracing the causes of labour and free love and atheism was shocking to American society back then. It was as if the greatest lawyer of today were to give public support to terrorism or paedophilia.

Darrow's advocacy for causes, both in and out of court, was genuine and heart-felt. He argued for causes, and he chose many of his cases to pursue those causes. One such case, admittedly an extreme example, was *Scopes v. Tennessee*. John Thomas Scopes had been charged under a Tennessee law that forbade teaching the theory of evolution. Darrow represented Scopes. This was the famous Monkey Trial. If a taste for the theatrical is part and parcel of advocacy, the Monkey Trial was pure theatre. As an agnostic and free thinker, the cause was irresistible to Darrow. He said, 'I do not pretend to know where many ignorant men are sure — that is all that agnosticism means.' In 1960, the trial was the subject of a film, *Inherit the Wind*, in which Spencer Tracy played Darrow.

Reading Darrow's life had a profound effect on me. Darrow practised law in order to achieve justice. He once said, 'Laws should be like clothes — they should be designed to fit the people they serve.'

THE SECOND Peloponnesian War started in 431 BC and ran for 27 years until 404 BC. It was a fight between Athens and the Peloponnesian League led by Sparta. Sparta won.

In about 415 BC, a delegation of Athenians visited the Island of Melos. Melos was located east of the Peloponnesian peninsula, and would therefore be strategically useful to the Athenians. They announced their intention to invade Melos, and conceded that they would do so without any claim of right. They explained:

> [Y]ou know as well as we do that right, as the world goes, is only in question between equals in power, while the strong do what they can, and the weak suffer what they must.

That simple idea is immediately recognisable: it is the law of the jungle, and still appears to inform international relations. Until relatively recent times — at least until the middle of the 18th century in England — it was a fair account of the way things worked in the English legal system.

The strong do what they can, and the weak suffer what they must.

The great project of modern legal systems is to temper the harshness of that idea: to ensure as far as possible that the weak as well as the strong will receive equal justice.

The purpose of this book is to explain how the legal system pursues that objective, and to suggest ways in which it might do so more effectively.

1

Foundations

Most Australians would, if asked, probably identify Magna Carta as the foundation stone of our legal system. They would have a vague sense that Magna Carta was the start of it in England and that, in 1788, the system built on Magna Carta was transplanted into Australia.

Magna Carta is mostly a myth, but it provides a great example of an enduring truth: in political matters, mythology is far more important than facts. Popular history tells us that Magna Carta was sealed on the meadow at Runnymede on 15 June 1215. So, on 15 June 2015, we commemorated 800 years since it was sealed. In fact, we acknowledged the wrong document and the wrong day.

The document that was sealed on 15 June 1215 was the Articles of the Barons. The document we think of as Magna Carta was based on the Articles of the Barons, and was prepared and engrossed a few days later — some say on 19 June 1215.

But, in any event, England switched from the Julian calendar to the Gregorian calendar in 1752, so as to bring the calendar back into synchronisation with the real world. When that switch happened, 11 days simply disappeared. So while it is true that the Articles of the Barons, later called Magna Carta, was signed on 15 June 1215, that day was 800 years minus 11 days before 15 June 2015. The date that is exactly 800 years after the signing of the Articles of the Barons was actually 26 June 2015.

But this does not matter: it is the symbolism of the thing that really counts, and I doubt that anyone thought about Magna Carta on 26 June 2015.

Winston Churchill wrote about the signing of Magna Carta in volume 1 of his great *A History of the English-Speaking Peoples*:

On a Monday morning in June, between Staines and Windsor, the barons and Churchmen began to collect on the great meadow at Runnymede. An uneasy hush fell on them from time to time. Many had failed to keep their tryst; and the bold few who had come knew that the King would never forgive this humiliation. He would hunt them down when he could, and the laymen at least were staking their lives in the cause they served. They had arranged a little throne for the King and a tent. The handful of resolute men had drawn up, it seems, a short document on parchment. Their retainers and the groups and squadrons of horsemen in sullen steel kept at some distance and well in the background. For was not armed rebellion against the Crown the supreme feudal crime? Then events followed rapidly. A small cavalcade appeared from the direction of Windsor. Gradually men made out the faces of the King, the Papal Legate, the Archbishop of Canterbury, and several bishops. They dismounted without ceremony. Someone, probably the Archbishop, stated briefly the terms that were suggested. The King declared at once that he agreed. He said the details should be arranged immediately in his chancery. The original 'Articles of the Barons' on which Magna Carta is based exist to-day in the British Museum. They were sealed in a quiet, short scene, which has become one of the most famous in our history, on June 15, 1215. Afterwards the King returned to Windsor. Four days later, probably, the Charter itself was engrossed. In future ages it was to be used as the foundation of principles and systems of government of which neither King John nor his nobles dreamed.

King John was the youngest of five sons of Henry II. His oldest brother, Richard, was king, but went off to fight the crusades, where he earned his nickname 'Lionheart'. John's other elder brothers, William, Henry, and Geoffrey, died young. Richard died in 1199, and John became king.

Richard and John both incurred huge expenses in war, especially in suppressing rebellion in their French domains in Normandy and Anjou. Both leaned on their nobles to support the expense. John, who had managed to make himself deeply unpopular, met resistance. He made increasing demands for taxes of various sorts, including scutage — money paid to avoid military service — and he sold wardships and heiresses for large sums. Henry II and Richard had done the same, but John's nobles resisted. By May 1215, the barons had occupied London and made a series of demands.

In June 1215, the barons met King John at Runnymede. The archbishop of Canterbury, Stephen Langton, played an important role in mediating the dispute, and eventually the Articles of the Barons were prepared and sealed.

Before it became known as Magna Carta, it was set aside. Two months after the Articles of the Barons were signed, King John (who was not a reliable person) prevailed on Pope Innocent III to declare the Deed invalid. The Pope said it was 'not only shameful and base but illegal and unjust'. He declared it null and void, and ordered King John not to observe it. This was in August 1215, just 10 weeks after the great symbolic meeting at Runnymede.

The barons were not happy.

John died in October 1216, when his son Henry was only nine years old. Henry's advisors saw that re-issuing the charter in modified form would help keep the young king in power. So an amended version was issued in 1217, under the title of the Charter of Liberties. At the same time, the Charter of the Forest was issued. The Charter of Liberties was the bigger of the two, and soon became known as the Great Charter: Magna Carta.

When he came of age, Henry III swore his allegiance to a

modified version of Magna Carta. This took place on 11 February 1225, so that is probably the most appropriate date to observe. The 1225 version of Magna Carta more closely resembles the document that has been so venerated for so long.

Perhaps people will celebrate the 800th anniversary of Magna Carta on 11 February 2025, or perhaps on 22 February 2025 to allow for the change in calendars. But probably not.

The 1215 version of Magna Carta includes many provisions that are concerned with taxes. For example:

(2) If any earl, baron, or other person that holds lands directly of the Crown, for military service, shall die, and at his death his heir shall be of full age and owe a 'relief', the heir shall have his inheritance on payment of the ancient scale of 'relief'.

(12) No 'scutage' or 'aid' may be levied in our kingdom without its general consent, unless it is for the ransom of our person, to make our eldest son a knight, and (once) to marry our eldest daughter. For these purposes only a reasonable 'aid' may be levied. 'Aids' from the city of London are to be treated similarly.

(15) In future we will allow no one to levy an 'aid' from his free men, except to ransom his person, to make his eldest son a knight, and (once) to marry his eldest daughter. For these purposes only a reasonable 'aid' may be levied.

(27) If a free man dies intestate, his movable goods are to be distributed by his next-of-kin and friends, under the supervision of the Church. The rights of his debtors are to be preserved.

(28) No constable or other royal official shall take corn or other movable goods from any man without immediate payment, unless the seller voluntarily offers postponement of this.

(30) No sheriff, royal official, or other person shall take horses or carts for transport from any free man, without his consent.

And there are plenty of surprises:

(4) The guardian of the land of an heir who is under age shall take from it only reasonable revenues, customary dues, and feudal services. ...

(5) For so long as a guardian has guardianship of such land, he shall maintain the houses, parks, fish preserves, ponds, mills, and everything else pertaining to it, from the revenues of the land itself. When the heir comes of age, he shall restore the whole land to him, stocked with plough teams and such implements of husbandry as the season demands and the revenues from the land can reasonably bear.

(6) Heirs may be given in marriage, but not to someone of lower social standing. Before a marriage takes place, it shall be made known to the heir's next-of-kin.

(10) If anyone who has borrowed a sum of money from Jews dies before the debt has been repaid, his heir shall pay no interest on the debt for so long as he remains under age, irrespective of whom he holds his lands. If such a debt falls into the hands of the Crown, it will take nothing except the principal sum specified in the bond.

(11) If a man dies owing money to Jews, his wife may have her dower and pay nothing towards the debt from it. If he leaves children that are under age, their needs may also be provided for on a scale appropriate to the size of his holding of lands. The debt is to be paid out of the residue, reserving the service due to his feudal lords. Debts owed to persons other than Jews are to be dealt with similarly.

(33) All fish-weirs shall be removed from the Thames, the Medway, and throughout the whole of England, except on the sea coast.

(35) There shall be standard measures of wine, ale, and corn (the London quarter), throughout the kingdom. There shall also be a standard width of dyed cloth, russett, and haberject, namely two ells[1] within the selvedges. Weights are to be standardised similarly.

The only part of Magna Carta that is widely remembered (if that is the right word) is found in Articles 39 and 40:

(39) No free man shall be seized or imprisoned, or stripped of his rights or possessions, or outlawed or exiled, or deprived of his standing in any other way, nor will we proceed with force against him, or send others to do so, except by the lawful judgment of his equals or by the law of the land.

(40) To no one will we sell, to no one deny or delay right or justice.

Together, these became Article 29 of the 1225 version:

(29) No free-man shall be taken, or imprisoned, or dispossessed, of his free tenement, or liberties, or free customs, or be outlawed, or exiled, or in any way destroyed; nor will we condemn him, nor will we commit him to prison, excepting by the legal judgment of his peers, or by the laws of the land. To none will we sell, to none will we deny, to none will we delay right or justice.

Considering the mystic significance that is attached to Magna

---

1 An ancient unit of measure, but not a very useful one in a standardised system, because its value varied from place to place. The English *ell* = 45 inches; the Scottish *ell* = 37·2 inches; the Flemish *ell* = 27 inches.

Carta these days, it is interesting to note that Shakespeare, in his play *King John*, does not mention it at all. He mentions Stephen Langton, the archbishop of Canterbury, who played a large part in compiling the document. But he mentions Langton just once, and in passing. He does not mention Runnymede.

SIR EDWARD COKE

So why do we honour it so greatly? The short answer is: Sir Edward Coke. And here we embark on a truly remarkable story of a new reality being formed as myth is piled on myth.

Sir Edward Coke (pronounced 'Cook') entered the English parliament in 1589, during the reign of Queen Elizabeth I. In 1594, he became attorney-general, and still held that role when James VI of Scotland became James I of England in 1603.

Elizabeth's father, Henry VIII, had famously broken from the Church of Rome because he wanted a divorce. The formation of the Church of England led to increasing oppression of English Catholics, which sharpened during the reign of Elizabeth. Elizabeth died without leaving an heir or any obvious successor, and when James VI of Scotland was cautiously chosen as Elizabeth's successor, the oppressed Roman Catholics of England had hopes that James might treat them more leniently. After all, James was married to Anne of Denmark who, although a Protestant, had converted to Catholicism.

But these hopes were dashed, and a group of well-educated, pious Catholic nobles conceived a bold plan to resist the increasing oppression: they would blow up the houses of parliament on the day of its opening. The opening of James' first parliament was delayed because the Plague had spread through London. For the opening, the Royal family, the Lords and the Commons would collect together in the Great Hall at Westminster. Eventually, the date was set for 5 November 1605. But word of the conspiracy got out. The night before parliament was due to open, the whole parliament building was searched. In a room immediately below the great hall, a man who called himself John Johnson was discovered. He had 36 barrels of gunpowder: enough to blow the whole place sky-high.

John Johnson was also known as Guy Fawkes.

King James personally authorised the torture of John Johnson, in an attempt to identify the other conspirators. Torture was unlawful then, as it is now. But King James considered that he ruled above the law. He adhered to the theory of the Divine Right of Kings. In this, we see the elemental force that was at play in the constitutional struggles of the 17th century. The key question was this: Does the King rule above the law, or is he subject to it?

The trial of the Gunpowder conspirators began on 26 January 1606. Sir Edward Coke, as attorney-general, prosecuted the case. He won. He was a favourite of King James because, on many occasions, he had supported King James's view that the King ruled above the law. Later in 1606 he was rewarded for his loyalty and good service by being appointed Chief Justice of Common Pleas.

On the bench, Coke's view seems to have changed. This sometimes happens to judges, to the great irritation of governments. In a number of cases, Coke CJ insisted that the King ruled subject to law. It is a principle we take for granted these days, but in the early 17th century it was hotly contested. He rejected King James's interference with the operation of the courts. The King dismissed him from office in 1616, whereupon he re-entered parliament.

THE PETITION OF RIGHT

In 1627 (the second year of the reign of Charles I) the King ordered the arrest of Sir Thomas Darnel and four others who had refused to advance a compulsory 'loan' to the King. They sought habeas corpus. The jailer answered the suit by saying the five were held '*per speciale mandatum Regis*' [by special order of the King].

Darnel's case in 1627 prompted Coke to draft for parliament the Petition of Right (1628). The petition raised, very politely, various complaints about the King's conduct, including that:

- he had been ordering people, like Darnel, to be jailed for failing to lend him money;
- he had been billeting soldiers in private houses throughout the country against the wishes of the owners;
- he had circumvented the common law by appointing commissioners to enforce martial laws and those commissioners had been summarily trying and executing 'such soldiers or mariners or other desolate persons joining with them as should commit ... (any) outrage or misdemeanour whatsoever ...'; and
- he had been exempting some from the operation of the common law.

The parliament prayed that the King 'would be graciously pleased for the further comfort and safety of your people, to declare ... that in the things aforesaid all your officers and ministers shall serve you according to the laws and statutes of this realm ...'.

The Petition of Right reflected Coke's distilled thoughts about English law and politics. In his most famous work, The *Institutes of the Lawes of England*, Coke elevated Magna Carta to previously unrecognised significance. He claimed that it was the source of all English law, and in particular he claimed it required that the King rule subject to law, not beyond it. He said that Magna Carta 'is such a fellow that he will have no sovereign'.

The Petition of Right was Coke's way of creating (he would have said 'recognising') the essential features of the English constitutional framework.

The Petition of Right was adopted by the parliament, but

Charles I would not agree to it. Charles I, like John centuries earlier, wanted to continue raising taxes without the inconvenience of having to seek parliamentary permission. Like King John, he did so by exacting large sums from his nobles, as he had done in Darnel's case. Again, the nobles were unhappy. The Civil War started in 1642. Charles lost the war and, in 1649, his head. Then came Cromwell, Charles II, and James II.

James II was a Catholic and was not popular. His son-in-law, William of Orange, was persuaded to usurp the throne of England. On 5 November 1688, in what became known as the 'Glorious Revolution', William landed at Brixham. That year, 5 November turned out worse for James II than it had in 1605 for James I. James was deposed, and William and Mary became joint sovereigns in James's place.

But there was a condition. William had agreed in advance to accept the Petition of Right. So the parliament of 1689 adopted the petition, and it became the English Bill of Rights. By this path, Sir Edward Coke's views on Magna Carta gained an unassailable place in the fabric of English law.

In form, the Bill of Rights declares itself to be 'An Act Declaring the Rights and Liberties of the Subject and Settling the Succession of the Crown'.

It recites and responds to the vices of James II. Its Preamble starts this way:

> Whereas the late King James the Second, by the assistance of divers evil counsellors, judges and ministers employed by him, did endeavour to subvert and extirpate the Protestant religion and the laws and liberties of this kingdom …

It then declares certain 'ancient rights and liberties'. The English Bill of Rights does, in some ways, reflect Magna Carta. So:

Magna Carta (1215) Article 12: No 'scutage' or 'aid' may be levied in our kingdom without its general consent, unless it is for the ransom of our person, to make our eldest son a knight, and (once) to marry our eldest daughter. For these purposes only a reasonable 'aid' may be levied. 'Aids' from the city of London are to be treated similarly.

Bill of Rights, clause 4: That levying money for or to the use of the Crown by pretence of prerogative, without grant of Parliament, for longer time, or in other manner than the same is or shall be granted, is illegal.

And the ideas underlying Article 20 of Magna Carta and clause 10 of the Bill of Rights are similar:

Magna Carta (1215) Article 20: For a trivial offence, a free man shall be fined only in proportion to the degree of his offence, and for a serious offence correspondingly, but not so heavily as to deprive him of his livelihood. In the same way, a merchant shall be spared his merchandise, and a husbandman the implements of his husbandry, if they fall upon the mercy of a royal court. None of these fines shall be imposed except by the assessment on oath of reputable men of the neighbourhood.

Bill of Rights, clause 10: That excessive bail ought not to be required, nor excessive fines imposed, nor cruel and unusual punishments inflicted;

Beyond this, other parallels can be found, but it takes the ingenuity of Sir Edward Coke to make them sound persuasive. For example, Article 61 of Magna Carta of 1215 (which was not repeated in the 1225 version adopted by Henry III) provides for a council of 25 barons to hold the King to his promises, and clause 13 of the Bill of Rights requires parliaments to be held frequently.

But Coke had persuaded a generation of lawyers and historians that the liberties in the Petition of Right, and thus in the Bill of Rights, were recognised in Magna Carta. So the importance of Magna Carta was picked up and sustained by the Bill of Rights.

THE US BILL OF RIGHTS

We do not think about the English Bill of Rights very much these days. When we hear a reference to the Bill of Rights, we automatically think of the United States of America. This is not an accident. The American colonies had been established by the English when they settled Jamestown in 1607. By 1773, things were not going well. The Boston Tea Party took place on 16 December; it was the colonists' protest against having to pay taxes to a distant government in which they had no representation. In 1776 the colonists decided to sever their ties with Britain, and on 4 July 1776 they signed the Declaration of Independence.

In 1789 a constitution was proposed for the newly independent United States of America. It was a bold and unprecedented venture. The idea of a federation of states with local as well as a central government was a novelty back then. The 13 colonies, anxious about the possible tyranny of a federal government, put forward 10 amendments to the constitution. Those amendments are known, in America and across the English-speaking world, as the Bill of Rights. They closely reflected the English Bill of Rights of 1689.

The parallels between the English Bill of Rights and the US Bill of Rights are very clear:

ENGLISH BILL OF RIGHTS (1689)	US BILL OF RIGHTS (1791)
Preamble: By raising and keeping a standing army within this kingdom in time of peace without consent of Parliament, and **quartering soldiers contrary to law**	5 - **No Soldier shall, in time of peace be quartered in any house,** without the consent of the Owner, nor in time of war, but in a manner to be prescribed by law.
3 - That the commission for **erecting the late Court of Commissioners for Ecclesiastical Causes,** and all other commissions and courts of like nature, are illegal and pernicious;	3 - **Congress shall make no law respecting an establishment of religion, or prohibiting the free exercise thereof;** or abridging the freedom of speech, or of the press; or the right of the people peaceably to assemble, and to petition the Government for a redress of grievances.
4 - That **levying money for or to the use of the Crown by pretence of prerogative,** without grant of Parliament, for longer time, or in other manner than the same is or shall be granted, is illegal;	See US constitution Article 1, Section 9 '… **No Money shall be drawn from the Treasury, but in Consequence of Appropriations made by Law;** and a regular Statement and Account of the Receipts and Expenditures of all public Money shall be published from time to time …'
7 - That the subjects which are **Protestants may have arms for their defence** suitable to their conditions and as allowed by law;	2 - A well-regulated Militia, being necessary to the security of a free State, **the right of the people to keep and bear Arms, shall not be infringed.**
10 - That excessive bail ought not to be required, nor excessive fines imposed, nor cruel and unusual punishments inflicted;	10 - Excessive bail shall not be required, nor excessive fines imposed, nor cruel and unusual punishments inflicted

5 - That **it is the right of the subjects to petition the king,** and all commitments and prosecutions for such petitioning are illegal;	3 - No law respecting an establishment of religion, or prohibiting the free exercise thereof; or abridging the freedom of speech, or of the press; or the right of the people peaceably to assemble, and **to petition the Government for a redress of grievances.**

Two important provisions of the US Bill of Rights reflect Articles 39 and 40 of the 1215 Magna Carta (Article 29 of the 1225 re-issue):

Magna Carta (1225) Art 29: No free-man shall be taken, or imprisoned, or dispossessed, of his free tenement, or liberties, or free customs, or be outlawed, or exiled, or in any way destroyed; nor will we condemn him, nor will we commit him to prison, excepting by the legal judgment of his peers, or by the laws of the land. To none will we sell, to none will we deny, to none will we delay right or justice.

Bill of Rights, clause 8: In all criminal prosecutions, the accused shall enjoy the right to a speedy and public trial, by an impartial jury … and to be informed of the nature and cause of the accusation; to be confronted with the witnesses against him; … and to have the Assistance of Counsel for his defence.

Bill of Rights, clause 9: the right of trial by jury shall be preserved, and no fact tried by a jury, shall be otherwise re-examined in any Court.

It is no great surprise that the American colonists drew so heavily on the English Bill of Rights. Sir Edward Coke's Petition of Right represented a stand against the Divine Right of Kings: it sought to place the ultimate law-making power in the people, through their elected representatives, and it sought to ensure that no one would stand above the law. The American colonists in 1789 were in the process of creating a new and powerful body that would hover above the various states. It looked as though they might be creating a new monarchy. To guard against this, they proposed the first 10 amendments to the proposed constitution.

The US Bill of Rights had very little to do with human rights. It was all about constraining the power of the new federal government.

THE PRINCIPLE OF LEGALITY

Article 29 of the 1225 version of Magna Carta is sufficient justification for the document's fame. Its provisions have since been taken to stand for the proposition that punishment can only be imposed by a court, that laws apply to all equally, and that all people are entitled to have their legal rights judged and declared by a court. This is more grandly expressed as the principle of legality or the rule of law.

In Australia, we did not adopt a bill of rights in our federal constitution, and our constitutional fathers did not have the same reasons to be anxious about a federal government as the American colonists had a century earlier. But the High Court of Australia has found in the structure of our constitution a principle of legality that reflects the spirit of Magna Carta as interpreted by Coke.

The Australian Constitution is divided into chapters. The first three create the parliament, the executive government, and the courts respectively. The High Court very early on decided that this gives each arm of government exclusive rights within its own domain. So, for example, only the parliament can exercise the legislative power, and only the courts can exercise the judicial power. For present purposes, this means that courts can impose punishment, but the parliament and the executive cannot. Parliament can pass a law that says, 'Doing x is illegal; penalty, five years' jail', but only a court can find that a person has done x, and impose the appropriate punishment.

At least according to Coke, this echoes the famous provision in Article 39 of Magna Carta that 'No free man shall be seized or imprisoned … except by the lawful judgment of his equals.'

It seems odd, and not a little ironic that, in the year of the 800th anniversary of Magna Carta, Australians were confronted with a government that seriously challenged the rule of law.

Here are three examples.

A Bill introduced into the federal parliament in 2015 authorised guards in immigration detention centres to treat detainees, including children, with such force as they thought was reasonably necessary. As a retired Court of Appeal judge said to a parliamentary enquiry, this would, in theory, allow a guard to beat a detainee to death without the risk of any civil or criminal sanction.

The Abbott government also advanced the idea that any Australian who goes to fight with the Islamic State should be stripped of his or her citizenship by a minister of the Crown — that is to say, by a member of the executive government. The measure was not adopted. However, the Australian Citizenship Act provides that a person aged 14 or older ceases to be an Australian citizen if he or she is a national or citizen of a country other than Australia and fights overseas for a declared terrorist organisation. The minister must give the person notice of the cessation. The person has the right to challenge the underlying facts, but that right may be less useful than it seems, because the minister can cancel the person's Australian passport — on the advice of the Australian Security Intelligence Organisation (ASIO), for example — and that would make it difficult or impossible for the person to return to Australia to challenge what has been done.

Having your citizenship cancelled looks very much like a

punishment, but the Abbott government was determined to be able to do this without troubling a court to see if the relevant facts were proved and the punishment was required by law. And, archaic as it seems, letting the minister take away a person's citizenship looks very much like outlawing or exiling the person without the judgment of his equals. It entails punishment without trial.

This is not a political argument: it is an argument about the rule of law, and is as serious and important as it was in 1215.

In the 21st century, it is too late to deny that Magna Carta has developed a level of significance that its authors may not have noticed or intended. If we are true to the spirit which Sir Edward Coke found in it; if we are true to the spirit that informed the Petition of Right and the English Bill of Rights and the American Bill of Rights, we owe it to the past and to the future to resist any attempt by any government to punish or outlaw or exile any person, except by the judgment of his equals.

2

Some basic concepts

Most Australians gain their understanding of the legal system by watching American TV shows like *Law and Order*, *LA Law*, and *Boston Legal*. Those shows might be a passably accurate account of the American system, but they do not reflect the Australian legal system at all.

In this chapter, I try to set out some of the basic ideas of the Australian legal system. But I repeat the warning given in the Introduction: this is not a DIY manual. It will not equip you with the ability to run or defend an action for yourself. Its only purpose is to enable you to understand some aspects of how the system works.

SOURCES OF LAW

Australian law was drawn initially from the English common law. When the Australian colonies formed a federation in 1901, the Commonwealth Constitution created the Commonwealth parliament, the Commonwealth executive, and the Commonwealth courts. The constitution confers specific powers on those three limbs of government, and sets limits to those powers.

Broadly speaking, the parliament's role is to make laws (by passing Acts of parliament); the role of the executive is to implement those laws; and the role of the courts is to resolve disputes arising from the laws and their implementation.

So, for example, the Commonwealth parliament might pass a law requiring all recreational fishermen to hold a fishing licence. The relevant government department — part of the executive arm of government — would then establish a mechanism for receiving fees, issuing licences, and policing the licence system to make sure that people who should have licences do hold them in fact.

Suppose a person is prosecuted for a breach of the fishing-licence law. He runs a fish-farming business, and is charged with hauling fish out of the artificial lake on his own property in which he has grown them. The matter goes to court. He says he didn't do anything — it was an employee of his who was hauling in the fish. He also argues that harvesting fish grown on a fish farm does not amount to 'fishing' within the meaning of the Act.

The court has to interpret the Act in order to see whether what was done is caught by the Act.

The defendant also argues that the Act goes beyond the power of the Commonwealth parliament, so the court has to decide whether — even if the defendant was 'fishing' as defined — the Act was a valid exercise of Commonwealth legislative power.

So the same set of facts gives rise to a factual question (Was it the defendant who was 'fishing?'); a question of statutory interpretation (Did what was done constitute 'fishing?'); and a constitutional question (Does the Commonwealth parliament have power to impose licence fees for the activity alleged?).

The hypothetical example of the fishing licence could result in either a civil or a criminal case. The distinction is important. A criminal case is one in which the state prosecutes a person for breaking a law that prohibits particular kinds of behaviour (for example, fishing without a licence), and prescribes penalties (such as a fine or a jail term) for a breach of that obligation.

Broadly stated, the criminal law is society's way of imposing norms of conduct and enforcing those norms by punishing those who are caught breaching them.

If the state is right in its arguments, the fishing-farm operator will be fined, and will probably make a point of getting a fishing licence in the future. If the state's arguments fail, the fishing-farm operator will be acquitted.

By contrast, a civil case is one in which citizens (or the state) can seek to vindicate their legal position in the courts. So the fish-farm operator could issue proceedings seeking a declaration that the state is acting without power in demanding that he obtain a fishing licence in the circumstances. If the fishing-farm operator is right, the court will declare that his operation does not require him to hold a licence, and might grant an injunction restraining the state from demanding payment of a licence fee.

Of course, the hypothetical fishing-licence example does not represent the average civil litigation, or the average criminal litigation.

Most civil cases concern claims for payment of debts, or compensation for damage done by someone's carelessness. Most criminal cases involve road-traffic offences or criminal assaults of one form or another. The most visible criminal cases (but among the least numerous) involve rape, very serious assault, or murder.

To the attentive reader, one thing will be immediately obvious: most (not all) cases involve at least two parties. In criminal cases, the state prosecutes, and the accused person defends. In civil litigation, one party asserts a right against the other; the plaintiff (or applicant) alleges a right, and the defendant (or respondent) contests the allegation.[1] As the hypothetical fishing-licence example shows, the bases of the defence can be factual ('the facts are not as you allege'); legal ('the law does not apply in the way alleged'); or constitutional ('the law, if it applies, is inconsistent with the constitution and is therefore invalid').

---

1   In most courts, the person complaining is called a plaintiff, or a complainant, or an applicant, and the opposite party is a defendant or respondent.

In the overwhelming majority of cases, it is the facts that dictate the outcome of the contest. In some cases (perhaps 5 per cent of them), a real question about the content or meaning or application of the law arises. In a very small number of cases, a constitutional question presents itself.

In the English legal tradition (which we inherited, as did America, India, and other former British colonies), we have the adversary system in litigation: one party asserts, and another party resists. The judge is an impartial umpire whose role it is to make sure things run according to the rules, and then to decide the factual and legal questions in the case. This is quite different from the European system, which gives judges a much more proactive role in proceedings.

Because our system pits the parties against each other, there is an ever-present risk that the parties will be unequal in resources. When the state is on one side of the contest, the mismatch is almost inevitable: the state is generally better resourced than most individuals or companies. Even when the contest is between individuals, there is always a risk that their resources will be mismatched — some times, grossly so.

Here lies one of the greatest failings of the system: resorting to the law is expensive, so a well-resourced litigant has an immense advantage over a less well-resourced opponent.

DIFFERENT KINDS OF LAW

Many lay people are confused by the distinction between various kinds of law. We regularly hear of civil law, criminal law, constitutional law, property law, and maybe even administrative law. And there are other sorts, probably less widely known.

The distinctions above cover several dimensions. Civil law can mean the law that operated in Roman times, but that is not what is usually meant. Civil law as distinct from criminal law is one of the basic distinctions

Criminal law is that set of rules which prohibit various forms of behaviour as undesirable in the interest of society as a whole. These are the rules that set out a citizen's obligations to the state. So: murder, careless driving, and so on are identified by the law as crimes, and the law identifies the punishment that may be imposed if a person is convicted of the relevant offence. When a person is charged with an offence against the criminal law, it is society's way of vindicating itself. If a fine is imposed, the proceeds generally go to the Crown.

Civil law is that body of rules which sets out the obligations of citizens to each other. If a person drives carelessly and, as a result, injures someone else, the driver faces the prospect of being charged with careless driving (penalty: a fine payable to the state), and in addition the driver can be sued for damages by the person who has been injured. On the criminal charge, the fact of careless driving has to be proved beyond reasonable doubt. On the civil claim, the fact of careless driving has only to be proved on the balance of probabilities: that is, is it more likely than not that the defendant did what is alleged?

The injured plaintiff will also have to prove, on the balance of probabilities, that the careless driving caused the loss he or she has suffered, and will have to prove the extent of that loss.

Similarly, if a person steals goods from another, the state will vindicate itself by charging the person with theft, and the person whose goods were stolen can bring a civil claim for trespass or conversion, seeking the return of the goods, or (depending on circumstances) damages for the value of the goods or a sum representing the loss associated with the loss of the goods.

Common law is often heard about. The common law is the body of law that was developed over centuries by English judges. Parliament can pass statutes that override the common law, and they do this with increasing frequency, although generally in the guise of codifying it.

Constitutional law, in Australia, is law concerning the meaning and effect of the Australian Constitution. Not all countries have a written constitution (Britain, for example, does not), but Australia does. It is the most basic law of the land, which in 1901 set out the subject matters about which the federal parliament could make laws. It also established that state parliaments cannot pass laws that are the province of the federal parliament. The constitution cannot be changed, except by referendum. Historically, Australians have been reluctant to vote in favour of changing it.

If the High Court (which is the ultimate court in the Australian legal system) decides that an Act of the federal parliament goes beyond the limits set by the constitution, the effect is that the Act becomes invalid from the outset. Likewise, if the High Court decides that an Act of a state parliament intrudes on an area about which the federal parliament has passed a valid law, the state Act is, to that extent, invalid.

As mentioned in chapter 2, the Commonwealth Constitution is divided into chapters. The three arms of government (legislative, executive, and judicial) are each created by their own chapter, and their powers are spelled out in the chapter that creates them. In an early case, the High Court held that this structure carried with it the implication that one arm of government cannot exercise the powers given to another arm of government. So, the legislative arm of government (the parliament) cannot exercise the judicial power; and the judicial arm of government (the courts) cannot exercise the legislative power. Although it is as subtle as it is chimerical, the Separation of Powers doctrine is often called on to prevent the executive arm of government from punishing people, as punishment is central to the judicial power.

PLEADINGS

'Pleadings' is the generic term for the documents in which a claim and the defence against it are set out. The initiating document is generally called a Statement of Claim (or something to that effect), and the response is generally called a Defence. Depending on circumstances, there may be a Reply. Sometimes there is a Counterclaim, in which the defendant says (in substance), 'Even if I am liable as the plaintiff says, I have a claim against him that can be set off against his claim.' Sometimes there is a Third Party Notice, which brings into the litigation a person who is not already a party, and seeks to shift the blame onto them.

It is not difficult to see the potential for complexity here. Unfortunately, lawyers too often allow the potential to blossom, with the result that proceedings become needlessly complicated and correspondingly expensive. Most jurisdictions now have rules that punish a litigant who makes the litigation unnecessarily complex.

Lawyers generally have a reputation for being blinkered, dull, and pedantic. In the taxonomy of charisma, we generally rank somewhere between bank tellers and undertakers. Of course, this is wholly unjustified and has come about only because of the way we behave. For example, consider the way lawyers draft documents. Lawyers often fill documents (even straightforward documents) with chunks of dull boilerplate; we use language that has a closer affinity to the King James' version of the Bible than to contemporary English. In the memorable words of Brooking J. in *FAI Traders v. Savoy Plaza*:

> The lease of the Savoy tavern in Spencer Street suffers from the corpulence which seems to afflict all hotel leases. It runs for some 60 pages. When we open it, the lease exudes the faintly musty smell we have come to associate with leases of hotels. Cesspools and

distemper, graining and varnishing, are preserved in its covenants as reminders of a bygone age.[2]

Not only do we use antiquated language, but we seem also to excel in so twisting our thoughts that the thicket of words becomes impenetrable even to the most intrepid traveller. Lord Justice MacKinnon might have been referring to almost any lawyer's efforts when he wrote his judgment in *Winchester Court Limited v. Miller*. He was delivering the first judgment. Lord Justice Luxmoore was also on the bench, and was to deliver the second judgment:

> He must be a bold, if not a conceited, man who can feel confidence in forming, or expressing, an opinion on any one of the innumerable problems that arise out of what may be cited together as the 'rent and mortgage interest restriction acts' but, having once more groped my way about that chaos of verbal darkness, I have come to the conclusion, with all becoming diffidence, that the County Court Judge was wrong in this case. My diffidence is increased by finding that my brother Luxmoore has groped his way to the contrary conclusion.[3]

It is a commonplace that affidavits and pleadings are typically couched in language so opaque as to conceal rather than display the draftsman's ideas (if he had any). Simple propositions become contorted and encrusted, to the extent that reading them becomes unpalatable and, finally, impossible. Oddly, members of the public regard this as a mark of dull pedantry on the part of lawyers.

The average lawyer's lack of imagination is not confined to his or her homicidal assaults on the language. In their choice of strategy, many lawyers demonstrate a pedestrian way of thinking. Not just

---

2   (1993) 2 VR 434.
3   (1944) 1 KB 734 at 736.

in our documents, but also in our strategic thinking, lawyers tend to err on the side of dullness.

HOW THINGS GO WRONG

Consider the following, which might be the template on which a large proportion of modern civil litigation is based.

A couple decide to buy a milk bar. They make enquiries at the local estate agent. He takes them to a newly developed shopping centre, and assures them that Shop 13 is ideal for their purposes, because there will be 5,000 people a day passing through the shopping centre, and theirs will be the only milk bar in the area. But it turns out that he has just signed up two other tenants to operate convenience stores in the same centre, and the week before he received from the shopping-centre owner a recent demographic survey demonstrating that the freeway recently opened nearby would divert almost all of the passing trade from the shopping centre; accordingly, no more than 1,000 persons per day are likely to visit the shopping centre in the foreseeable future.

By the time the venture fails, as it must, the plaintiffs have lost $40,000 in lease payments and have earned $25,000 less income than they had budgeted for.

In the hands of many lawyers, this fairly commonplace set of facts results in a Statement of Claim seeking relief as follows:

- Misleading and deceptive conduct in contravention of the Consumer and Competition Act (previously known as the Trade Practices Act: a tag I will wilfully keep using).
- Misleading and deceptive conduct in contravention of the Fair Trading Act.
- Unconscionable conduct in contravention of the Trade Practices Act.

- Misleading conduct in relation to an interest in land in contravention of the Trade Practices Act.
- Negligence.
- Breach of fiduciary duty (that is, breach of a duty which comes with particular positions of trust).
- Contravention of various provisions of the Estate Agents Act.
- Allegations of aiding and abetting, counselling, and procuring are made against the employee of the real estate agency, the developers, the directors of the development company, the owners of the site, and the directors of the shopping-centre owner.
- Damages are claimed that are supported only by an inflated estimate of earnings for the next 150 years, and punitive and exemplary damages are also sought.

The claim is brought against the estate agent and the shopping-centre owner. Naturally, they cross-claim against each other.

The Statement of Claim is a work of the pleader's art: it is a treasure trove of convolution, hyperbole, and repetition. We lawyers have all encountered such documents.

The solicitors for the defendants understand perfectly well the substance of what is alleged against their respective clients. Nevertheless, they foreshadow at the first directions hearing that they will bring an application to strike out the Statement of Claim. With two sets of counsel to be heard debating the precise meaning of each phrase in 60 tightly packed pages, it is little wonder that the strike-out application takes a week to prepare and a full day to argue.

More in sorrow than in anger, the judge determines that numerous paragraphs of the Statement of Claim should be struck out.

The plaintiffs now retain senior counsel, since the defendant has retained senior counsel. She wrestles with the pleading, and (having close regard to the terms of the judgment striking out various parts of the Statement of Claim) manages to improve the pleading substantially. This, of course, does not satisfy the defendant, who again seeks to strike it out. After another expensive argument, further deficiencies in the Statement of Claim are detected and duly remedied.

Pausing here, the process has consumed in total something between three to six months' elapsed time (depending on the availability of judges), many days of lawyers' time, and a few days in court. The total cost is approaching $100,000. The fact that this exceeds the true loss of the plaintiffs is a matter of sublime indifference: after all, the true case, which was always apparent to everyone, has now been pleaded in such a way that it is apparent to everyone. If there were any aspects of the Statement of Claim that were real sources of difficulty, the defendants have helped the plaintiffs sort out those difficulties, so that the plaintiffs have the inestimable advantage of having clarified their own thinking about their case.

We have all seen this happen.

It is very common to see defendants mount repeated assaults on a Statement of Claim. No pleading is ever perfect. A pleading should be struck out if it is truly incomprehensible or if, on any reasonable reading of it, it discloses no cause of action known to the law.

It is a very different matter, however, to say that, because a paragraph in a Statement of Claim is capable of bearing more than a single meaning, you should seek to strike it out. First, it may be that the alternative meanings available are sufficiently close to each other that it makes no difference which is the true meaning intended. Second, it may be that one of the meanings available on the face of the document is so absurd that any reasonable reader would understand that the other meaning is the meaning truly intended. Third, the English language is riddled with words that bear more than a single meaning; it is difficult to construct a paragraph in which you cannot find nuances of language that produce ambiguity. This being so, the right question for the defendant's lawyer to ask is not, 'Can we find any ambiguities in the Statement of Claim that we can attack?', but rather, 'What will be achieved by attacking the Statement of Claim?' In most cases, the only positive thing achieved by attacking the Statement of Claim is that the plaintiff's thinking becomes increasingly focussed, and their way of putting their case becomes more effective as its nuances are explored in the course of a strike-out application. It is difficult to see what line of reasoning dictates the strategic approach so often seen.

Naturally, when attacks on the Statement of Claim have run their course, the shopping-centre owners are required to file a defence. They deny the misleading conduct, but in any event they say that, even if it happened, it was the letting agent's fault. Filled with righteous indignation, they join the letting agent on a third-party claim.

The complexity of the defence and the cross-claims inevitably reflects the complexity of the Statement of Claim.

Where the stakes are high enough, a case may end up with a plaintiff, several defendants, a handful of third parties, and another handful of fourth parties, all bound together by a series of claims, cross-claims, and counter-claims so as to resemble a legal Gordian knot. Most practitioners who practise in commercial litigation will have had experience of cases in which there were one or two dozen solicitors, a similar number of barristers, and legal costs running up at one thousand dollars a minute.

COSTS

In civil litigation, the losing party is generally ordered to pay the costs of the successful party.

Litigation is expensive. This is partly because lawyering, like other professional activities, is a skilled occupation, and not everyone is able to do it. Lawyers charge a lot to do what they do, although their charge-out rate varies pretty widely. This is also true for pop singers and professional sports people.

That said, the cost of litigation can, and often does, come to dominate the way the litigation runs. Take the hypothetical milk-bar case discussed earlier. Suppose the defendants are determined to resist the claim, because they believe it is a try-on, and they are filled with righteous indignation. And they do not want other tenants in the unsuccessful shopping centre to bring similar claims.

Well-resourced litigants can make things complicated and expensive. While they may claim to be animated by the principle of not bowing to spurious claims, they also think they can run the plaintiffs into the ground by outspending them.

But suppose the damages claim is, initially, for only $65,000. 'Only $65,000'. For the disappointed milk-bar owners, it's a huge sum. But if the defendants fight it as outlined earlier, it will not be long before lawyers' fees of $65,000 have been run up. And if the case goes to trial, it will take two or three days, and, at the end, one side will lose. The losing side will not only have to pay its own costs, but will be ordered to pay the costs of the other party. The total bill will certainly come out somewhere north of $150,000.

In this way, the concept that justice is available to everyone on equal terms begins to look rather hollow. It was once noted, by an English judge, that the courts of British justice are 'open to every one (like the Savoy Hotel)'.

ACCESS TO JUSTICE: LEGAL AID

In civil litigation, Legal Aid is effectively unavailable. Presumably, this is because funding bodies consider fights about money and property less important than fights about children and crime. Other aspects of our social arrangements suggest a much greater concern for money and property than Legal Aid funding suggests. The absence of Legal Aid in civil litigation can work profound injustice, especially when the other litigants can afford their own lawyers. When one party is a well-resourced company, the individual litigant's rights are irrelevant: they will almost certainly have to sacrifice their rights because they cannot afford to vindicate them.

Tenancy disputes, consumer disputes, and credit disputes all have a profound impact on the affected litigant. To deny them access to Legal Aid is to subject them to the near certainty of injustice.

Civil litigation, of course, can involve questions that go beyond money and property. Discrimination and employment law are two examples. Victims of unlawful discrimination are doubly disadvantaged if they cannot get legal help to address the wrong already suffered.

Refugee cases are another obvious example where Legal Aid funding is, for practical purposes, not available. This is an area where grave injustices are being wrought every day. The reason for this is partly structural. As most people know, the process for seeking asylum is as follows. When the person arrives in Australia and seeks asylum, he or she tells their story to an officer of the immigration department. The officer decides whether to believe the story and, if so, whether the story makes out a valid claim for refugee status. If applicants are refused, they can appeal. Until 2013, the appeal was to the Refugee Review Tribunal (RRT). Then it was to an 'Independent Merits Reviewer'. Now it is to the Administrative Appeals Tribunal.

The quality of 'justice' dispensed by the RRT was quite distinctive. The RRT members did not have to be lawyers. They were appointed for a short term (a maximum of five years, but typically shorter than that), but they could be reappointed. If their decisions pleased the government, their chances of reappointment appeared to improve. Applicants were not entitled to be legally represented at RRT hearings. The decisions of the RRT were often literally a matter of life or death, and yet the decisions of the tribunal were almost completely immune to correction by a court. The Migration Act did not prescribe any qualification requirements for membership of the RRT. Its members might or might not have been lawyers. They might or might not have been university graduates in any discipline. Although it was called a tribunal, members sat alone: there was no one sitting beside them to catch errors or correct for biases. Appeals are now heard by the Administrative Appeals Tribunal (AAT). When hearing refugee appeals, AAT members sit alone.

Until late 2001, the Migration Act contained a provision to the effect that a decision of the RRT could not be overturned by a court merely because it contained an error of law, or because it was so unreasonable that no reasonable person could have made it. Buoyed by public enthusiasm over the handling of the Tampa episode, the Howard government introduced the 'privative clause' that, on its face, prevents any court from overturning any decision of the RRT on any grounds whatever. In fact, the effect of a privative clause does not quite match its grim promise, and the High Court in the case of *S157* construed the privative clause in such a way as to leave open the possibility of reviewing jurisdictional errors made by the RRT.[4]

I mention these things because they enable you to understand, even if only faintly, the feelings of failed asylum applicants who seek to have their cases reviewed in the courts: they have been subjected to a process that in many cases is plainly unfair, in a legal system that they almost certainly do not understand. While this process occurs, they have been detained in a jail in the desert, or in Nauru or Manus Island, even though they have never committed any offence. (See chapter 7.) For such people, there can be no possibility of thinking that they have received justice.

---

4   *Plaintiff S157/2002 v Commonwealth* [2003] HCA 2; 211 CLR 476.

In those circumstances, they are cast headlong, and without legal support, into the mysteries of administrative law and the rarefied atmosphere of the Federal Court or the High Court. While the courts are making a genuine effort to deal with the human tragedy of these circumstances, to think of this as 'access to justice' is delusional.

Politicians who are very keen on justice at election time tend to lose their enthusiasm for it when Legal Aid funding is in question. They overlook, or perhaps they don't realise, that most people can't navigate the legal system without the help of a lawyer, and that a lot of people can't afford a lawyer.

If a person is unlucky enough to find themselves enmeshed in the legal system, promises of justice sound hollow if a lawyer is beyond reach. It is a sorry thing to admit, but justice is only safely available to people who can afford a lawyer, and for many that means Legal Aid is essential if justice is to be achieved.

A former chief justice of Australia, Gleeson CJ, once said:

> The expense which Governments incur in funding Legal Aid is obvious and measurable, but what is real and substantial is the cost of the delay, disruption and inefficiency which results from the absence or denial of legal representation. Much of that cost is also borne, directly or indirectly, by Governments. Providing Legal Aid is costly. So is not providing Legal Aid.

Every litigant is entitled to participate without the help of a lawyer, but this is generally not a good idea, and it does not help the functioning of the system. The time needed for the case is extended when the unrepresented litigant needs, in effect, on-the-job training by the court. Judges and magistrates are generally astute enough to ensure that the unrepresented party is not disadvantaged unduly — but this takes time. The system would probably run more cost-effectively if every litigant were represented, even if the state payed for their representation.

Denying Legal Aid, and thus denying representation, will very likely prove to be a false economy in many cases.

But there is another cost — more difficult to quantify, but real enough. It is the damage done to the fabric of society itself when a growing number of people believe that they have been denied justice. This will be the response in most cases of unrepresented litigants — especially litigants who have sought, but have been refused, Legal Aid.

The consequences of this will be various. First, the individual is likely to think that the entire justice system is flawed. Taken together with other forces, this can be seriously damaging to the system itself. The justice system depends, at least in part, on a shared belief that it works. Without that shared belief, the system loses much of its authority. It is interesting to see in recent years an increasing tendency in the press to criticise judges, courts, and their decisions — especially sentencing decisions. In parallel, there is an increasing tendency for governments to also criticise judges, courts, and their decisions — especially in constitutional matters. In addition, governments have tended in recent years to show less respect for judges than was previously the case. This is seen, for example, in some governments suggesting that the 'productivity' of judges should be assessed, and that in various ways judges should be treated as simply another branch of the public service.

While no one would wish to see judges placed beyond the reach of control or criticism, these influences damage the authority of the courts. Against the background of such criticism, every unrepresented litigant will come away from court with his or her previous faith in the system further damaged. The cumulative effect of this is incalculable, and is undoubtedly harmful.

3

The justice system
and the legal system

W e refer without much hesitation to 'the justice system' and 'the legal system' as if they were identical. They are not. We have a legal system. Its objective is to produce justice as far as human wit can manage it. It is an imperfect system, as most human systems are.

This is not necessarily the fault of legal practitioners. They are, for the most part, simply the mechanics who tend and implement the system for the benefit of their clients. To understand how the system works, and the role of lawyers in it, it is necessary to understand a few of the basic elements of the system.

A SET OF RULES

The law is a set of rules. The rules are intended to cover all aspects of our existence and activity. The rules have different origins.

The common law is a body of rules built up over centuries by judges deciding individual cases. A person buys a carriage which turns out to have a defective wheel; the wheel collapses, and the owner and his goods are damaged. Is the vendor, or the manufacturer, liable for the damage? Or are they both liable? A person buys a soft-drink for his friend; she drinks it and becomes ill because it was contaminated during the manufacturing process. Is the vendor liable to her, even though she was not a party to the contract by which the drink was bought? A horse runs amok in the market place, causing injuries and damaging property: who is liable for the damage caused? A landowner produces noxious fumes on his land that cause injury and inconvenience to other landowners nearby: is he liable to them for the lawful use of his own land?

These are all examples of problems that common-law judges have dealt with over the centuries. As far as possible, judges try to decide cases in a way that is consistent with earlier judgments on equivalent facts. By that means, they make it possible to know in advance the legal consequences of proposed conduct. More or less.

The common-law rules evolved from case to case, but sometimes produced results that were demonstrably harsh. The Courts of Equity, run by the chancellor of the exchequer, devised a series of rules designed to relieve a litigant of the harsh operation of the common law. Equity operated on the conscience of the litigant, so that Equity might prevent a person making unconscionable use of his common-law rights. A significant modern example was a woman who had mortgaged her home as security for her son's loan from the bank. She was old, uneducated, and had limited English. Her son had not explained the significance of the transaction. The bank knew this. The son defaulted, and the bank wanted to seize the mother's house and sell it. It had a clear legal right to sell the house: the signed mortgage gave it that right, but, applying the principles of Equity, the court refused to allow the bank to sell the house.

Statutes are laws written by the parliament. Since about the middle of the 17th century in the English legal system, parliament has been the supreme law-maker. Subject to constitutional restraints, the parliament can make any laws it wants to. If the parliament passes a law which says that all blue-eyed babies should be killed at birth, that law would be valid (again, subject to constitutional restraints). It would be a terrible law, but a valid one. The laws that provide for the indefinite detention of refugees who arrive in Australia as boat people are an example of valid laws that produce harsh — even brutal — results. I discuss both of these matters later.

Parliaments make laws at a tremendous rate these days. In 1950, all the statutes of the Commonwealth parliament from Federation up to 1950 were consolidated in just four volumes. These days, the Commonwealth parliament produces at least two volumes of new legislation each year.

THE RULE-MAKERS

Increasingly, the rules are made by parliaments. In Australia, we have a parliament in each state and territory, and we have the Commonwealth parliament. At the time of Federation (1901), the colonies became states, and the Commonwealth was created over the top. This means that we have two overlapping systems of law-makers (parliaments).

The Commonwealth Constitution created the Commonwealth parliament, the executive government of the Commonwealth, and the federal judiciary. This means that we have two overlapping systems of law-enforcers (courts).

This is important, because the constitution sets limits on what the Commonwealth parliament can do.

The Commonwealth has a constitution. Each state also has a constitution. The powers of the states are limited by the powers of the Commonwealth parliament: where the Commonwealth has made a law within its constitutional power, the state cannot make a law inconsistent with the Commonwealth law.

ENFORCING THE RULES

On occasions, a parliament makes rules (that is, passes a statute) that go beyond the power given to it by the constitution. If parliament thinks it has power to make a particular rule, but someone disagrees, who is to be the referee? The answer is: the courts.

Courts deal with many sorts of disputes, but generally they are disputes between citizen and citizen, or between citizen and state. (From this point on, when I refer to 'the state', I generally mean the political entity relevant in the context, so it could be a reference to any of the states or territories, or to the Commonwealth. Generally, the term is used to distinguish between the citizen and the polity of which the citizen is a member.)

For example, if a person is run down by a car and suffers injuries, there may be several disputes which come before courts. First, if there is a civil dispute between the injured pedestrian and the driver of the car, a court will have to decide whether the driver was negligent, and if so what amount of money is appropriate compensation for the injuries. The end result, if the plaintiff succeeds, will be a judgment for a sum of money to be paid by the defendant to the plaintiff.

Second, the police may prosecute the driver for careless driving, driving while exceeding the prescribed blood-alcohol limit, and so on. If the prosecution succeeds, the result will be a form of punishment: the driver may be sentenced to a term of imprisonment, or have his licence cancelled, or be ordered to pay a fine to the state.

There are two principal differences between these actions. The civil action is a private action to vindicate the rights of the injured pedestrian. The court has to decide factual questions on the balance of probabilities: that is, the court has to decide whether it is more probable than not that a disputed fact is true.

The criminal prosecution is an action between the state and the citizen (the driver). The purpose is to enforce the body of rules comprising the criminal law, not to vindicate the rights of the injured pedestrian, but to uphold the criminal law and thereby (at least in theory) make the state safer for all citizens.

LITIGATION

All lawyers imagine that most people understand what litigation is. In fact, most people don't know what litigation is or how it works.

In the broadest sense, litigation is a dispute in the court system. It typically refers to civil cases rather than criminal cases. Although the words by which the various steps are described vary, most civil litigation has the same elements.

- The parties: the party who issues proceedings is typically called the plaintiff or the applicant. The party who has been sued is typically called the defendant or the respondent.
- The document by which litigation is started is typically called a Writ or a Summons or an Application. It is typically supported by a statement of what the plaintiff alleges are the facts giving rise to the problem, and the relief sought. That document is typically called the Statement of Claim. The defendant is required to respond to it, point by point, in a document typically called a Defence.
- The time between the issue of the Writ and the trial of the action is marked by a series of 'interlocutory' steps: this can include one party asking the other for 'further and better particulars' of the Statement of Claim or the Defence, and usually involves the parties disclosing the documents they have that are relevant to the issues in the case. This process is called 'discovery'.
- The interlocutory steps are typically ordered at one or more Directions Hearings: hearings in front of the judge whose

docket the case is on, or who manages the list the case is in, or who otherwise has some responsibility for the management of the case. There was a time when the parties would make their own pace in progressing through the interlocutory stages, but those days are long gone. Charles Dickens mocked the law's delay in *Bleak House*. What happened in *Bleak House* is unlikely to be tolerated or even possible in today's court system.

- Before the case goes to trial, it is increasingly common for the judge managing the case to order that the case go to mediation. The mediation is often conducted by a court officer who will disclose nothing about the mediation to the judge beyond whether or not the case resolved, because everything said in the course of a mediation is confidential. Mediation is a guided, structured negotiation between the warring parties. It is often a very successful way of resolving a dispute, except in those rare cases where the question depends primarily on a disputed question of law. The reason it is successful is that a skilled mediator can introduce elements into the mediation that are simply not available to the judge.

  For example: the plaintiff claims that the defendant took, and disposed of, a valuable piece of furniture owned by the plaintiff. The plaintiff seeks damages. The plaintiff and the defendant are brothers. At mediation, the mediator recognises that the plaintiff received the furniture under his mother's Will. The defendant is upset because he received shares, but nothing personal, under his mother's Will. The plaintiff is not much interested in the personal possessions he inherited, but is interested in shares. From that point, it's all horse-trading. Of course, even if the judge learned these background facts at trial, she would not be able to order a share-swap in exchange for personal items inherited by the plaintiff.

- The trial of the action is where the rubber hits the road. Witnesses give evidence; they are cross-examined; counsel make submissions back and forth. Then, when all the fun is over, the judge has to go and write a judgment. That usually involves deciding which witnesses should be believed; what facts should be found to have occurred; and what the law requires where those facts have occurred.
- If one party is very unhappy with the result, they can appeal it. (It has been said that the best judgment leaves both parties unhappy.) Appeals look at the record of the trial to see whether the trial judge made errors of law. Occasionally, an appeal court will disagree with a trial judge's findings of fact, but this is rare.
- Whether the case has gone through the state court system or the Federal Court system, the next available step is the High Court of Australia. But you can't appeal to the High Court as of right. You have to get special leave to appeal. It's not enough that the High Court thinks the decision of the court below was wrong: it must think there is a question of general importance at issue.

JUSTICE

Most people have a sense of what justice is, but it is not as easily understood as you might think. Here is a simple thought-experiment to see whether you understand justice:

A mother has had a hard day.

Her three children, but especially the youngest, are giving her a difficult time.

She is in the kitchen when she hears a crash in the front room.

She runs in to find her favourite, and very valuable, vase

smashed to pieces on the hearth.

She knows, with a certainty which brooks no contradiction, that the youngest is to blame. She punishes him severely, and sends him to bed without dinner.

As it happens, he was the one responsible for breaking the vase.

A variation:

A mother has had a hard day.

Her three children, but especially the youngest are giving her a difficult time.

She is in the kitchen when she hears a crash in the front room.

She runs in to find her favourite, and very valuable, vase smashed to pieces on the hearth.

She approaches each child in turn, and asks questions calculated to find out who was responsible. Taking everything into account, she decides that it was the youngest.

She punishes him severely, and sends him to bed without dinner.

As it happens, it was not him.

Which result is more just? Which instance comes closer to your sense of justice? Most people cannot give a quick answer. By their hesitation, they show that justice has at least two components: the result and the process. We can readily spot an unfair result; but equally we can easily see when a bad process has been used.

American legal dramas on TV often talk about due process. The American Bill of Rights includes a 'due process' clause in the Fifth Amendment, which explains why they talk of it so much.[1]

---

1 Clause 5 of the US Bill of Rights. The draft US Constitution was put forward in 1788 to the 13 colonies, which suggested 10 amendments to the documents. For a more detailed discussion, see chapter 2 and Appendix 4. The US Bill of Rights comprises the first 10 Amendments to the Constitution.

Most people with a sense of justice recognise that the process of applying the rules should be a fair one.

Recognising this fact has a downside: procedural rules grow up and become ever more complex, so that it can be very difficult navigating your way through procedural thickets to reach the destination of a just result.

BAIL

When a person is charged with a serious offence, they will either be remanded in custody or they may be granted bail.

On Friday 20 January 2017, a horrific incident happened in the Bourke St Mall in Melbourne. Dimitrious Gargasoulas allegedly drove his car into a group of pedestrians. Six people died: Matthew Si, aged 33; Jess Mudie, aged 22; Thalia Hakin, aged 10; three-month-old Zachary Bryant; a 25-year-old Japanese student who had only been in Australia for a little over a year; and Bhavita Patel, aged 33.

At the time of this event, Gargasoulas was on bail. He had been granted bail on 14 January for the alleged assault of his mother's partner. Police had opposed bail. He was later charged with five counts of murder.

The terrible events of 20 January 2017 ignited a debate about the grant of bail. The Melbourne *Herald Sun* ran an article under the headline: 'Bail must be automatically denied to people charged with serious offences, police say.'

Although the sentiment was attributed to police, the first paragraph of the story read:

UPDATE: THE presumption of bail should be removed for Victorians who are alleged to have committed violent offences, the state opposition says.

It later quoted the leader of the opposition in Victoria, Matthew Guy:

'The first principle is to introduce the presumption of remand for those charged with violent offences,' he said.

It was interesting, if not surprising, that the debate about bail was triggered by Gargasoulas's behaviour on 20 January, rather than by his being granted bail on 14 January. Presumably, bail was granted because it was thought that he would not offend while on bail. Sadly, that optimism was misplaced.

But the Bourke St Mall episode helped focus attention on the exceptionally difficult problem of bail, which involves reconciling several deep-seated principles with our concern to avoid terrible crimes.

The first principle is the presumption of innocence. This is fundamental to the operation of the English legal system, and is a central assumption of the Australian criminal-justice system: a person charged with an offence is presumed innocent until they are convicted of that offence. (See chapter 5.) The presumption of innocence is consistent with the principle that a person will not be convicted unless found guilty beyond reasonable doubt. The presumption of innocence and the criminal standard of proof beyond reasonable doubt are both intended to tilt the scales in favour of the accused. Both are deeply rooted in our system: they go back so far that it would be genuinely revolutionary to remove either.

But when a person commits an offence while on bail, the public, understandably, think that the offence would not have been committed if bail had been refused. That is almost certainly true, but misses the main point: our system of criminal justice is designed to punish people who have committed an offence. It is not designed to incarcerate a person because they might commit an offence at some time in the future.

The presumption of innocence is important when a person is charged with a serious offence. If they are remanded in custody pending trial, they will probably have to spend many months in jail before they are tried. When tried, they may be acquitted. If that happens, the accused will have been jailed for months despite being innocent, as they are presumed to be.

The injustice of jailing an innocent person is too obvious to need explanation.

The Victorian Bail Act provides that any person accused of an offence and being held in custody in relation to that offence must be granted bail, except in certain circumstances:

- Bail will be refused if the accused is charged with murder, treason, or various drug offences, unless the accused can show exceptional circumstances;
- Bail will be refused if the accused is charged with a terrorist offence, unless the court is satisfied that exceptional circumstances exist which justify the grant of bail; and
- Bail will be refused if the court considers that there is an unacceptable risk that the accused would skip bail, or would commit an offence while on bail, or would endanger the health or safety of the public, or would interfere with witnesses pending trial.

Obviously, if the Crown case against the accused is very strong, the refusal of bail does not carry much risk that the person will later be acquitted.

However, if the alleged offence is very serious, or the accused appears to be a danger to the community, remanding the person in custody may mean that an innocent person will be held in custody for many months. In cases such as this, the system is being used to deprive a person of their liberty just in case they commit an offence. It may seem attractive that we can prevent potential criminal offences by a person who is presumed innocent of the immediate charge but who is thought to be a risk generally, but that is not consistent with the basic assumptions of the system. Indeed, it is characteristic of the worst aspects of a police state that a person can be jailed 'just in case'.

The public debate that was triggered by the terrible events of 20 January 2017 in Melbourne was premised on the assumption that Dimitrious Gargasoulas should not have been granted bail. That proposition rests largely on the wisdom of hindsight. Of course, what he did was terrible. Of course, if he had been in custody he could not have done what he did. Of course, the public (and especially the tabloid media) are outraged when terrible things like this happen.

But the problem has to be addressed at the time bail is sought — at a time before the later offence is committed. That is the dilemma facing a court asked to grant or refuse bail. At that point, the court is dealing with a person who is presumed to be innocent. At that point, the court is asked to jail a person who might never be convicted. At that point, the court is invited to jail a person just in case they might commit an offence later, while on bail.

The law allows the court to consider the risk of the accused offending while on bail; but it does not have the benefit of hindsight. Criticism of the bail system in cases such as Gargasoulas's depends wholly on the benefit of hindsight.

As I write this, details are emerging of a terrible event that happened in London. On 22 March 2017, a man drove into a crowd of pedestrians on Westminster Bridge, killing four of them. Forty other pedestrians were injured. The driver later drove into the barrier outside the Parliament building and attacked and killed a policeman, and was himself killed. The episode had a grim resemblance to the Gargasoulas offence in Melbourne two months earlier. But the English offender was not on bail; so far as we know, he was not on anyone's radar as likely to commit such an offence.

UK police say the offender acted alone but was motivated by terrorism; Gargasoulas was not motivated by terrorism.

It is interesting to speculate on the public response if the government introduced a law which said that a person can be held in prison for up to 12 months if the police believe that the person might otherwise commit a criminal offence during that time. I hope that most people would think that a law such as this would be completely unacceptable: after all, isn't punishment what we do to people who are proved, at trial, to have committed a specific offence at a specific time in the past? The possibility of police jailing a person 'just in case' represents a greater threat to society than the madness of a few people who commit offences that might not have been committed if they were held in custody.

The bail system tries to reconcile competing values. Generally, it does this fairly well.

THE SYSTEM

The legal system, then, is a set of complex rules, enforced by a hierarchy of human actors, and governed by a complex set of procedural regulations. It is a system that creates rules and enforces them.

The main players are parliaments and lawyers. As noted above, parliaments make most of the rules.

'Lawyers' includes judges and legal practitioners. Judges decide how the rules are to be applied.

Legal practitioners (solicitors and barristers) try to persuade judges what the rules are, what they mean, and how they should be applied.

The end result of all this is justice. At least, that is the goal. Sometimes things go wrong along the way.

The court hierarchy

The usual hierarchy of state and territory courts in Australia is:

- Court of Appeal (it is a part of the Supreme Court; in some states it is called the Full Court)
- Supreme Court
- District Court (in Victoria, it is called the County Court)
- Magistrates Court

The hierarchy of federal courts in Australia is:

- High Court of Australia
- Full Court (of the Federal Court or Family Court)
- Federal Court of Australia and Family Court of Australia (they stand as equivalent in status, but with jurisdiction over different areas of law)
- Federal Circuit Court (previously known as the Federal Magistrates Court)

From the appeal level of each of the federal courts, and from the appeal division of each state and territory Supreme Court, there is a right to seek special leave to appeal to the High Court of Australia.

Some litigants find it maddening to learn that they cannot go to the High Court when they think the court below was wrong. There is a practical reason: the High Court would not be able to manage the case-load if every disappointed litigant could appeal to it as of right. Consequently, the court has a filtering mechanism: any disappointed litigant can seek special leave to appeal to the High Court, but only a small proportion get it. The High Court will typically grant special leave only in cases of general importance.

The fact that the court below got it wrong is *not* enough by itself to get a grant of special leave.

Judges

Typically, judges are lawyers who have been successful in legal practice. For a long time, judges were generally appointed from the ranks of the bar. In recent years, solicitors have been appointed to the bench. When a solicitor was first appointed as a judge of the Supreme Court of Victoria, some Victorian barristers reacted as if the sky had fallen in. That controversial appointment, of Justice Bernie Teague in 1987, turned out well. Teague J had a distinguished career as Supreme Court judge from 1987 until his retirement in 2008. Most barristers agree that he was a good judge, despite their earlier misgivings.

The key thing about judicial appointments is that judges need to know how trials work. That means they need a lot of trial experience. Until 1987, the received wisdom was that you could only learn to understand litigation from counsel's side of the bar table.

Judges are the most important people in the Australian legal system. It is their role to hear cases, decide which version of the facts they accept, and then decide the legal consequences of those facts.

The most significant feature of judges in the Australian legal system is that they are, both in theory and in practice, independent of government. This is of fundamental importance to the operation of the system. When a judge is appointed, he or she has tenure until they reach 70 years of age. Until they reach that age ('the age of statutory senility'), they can only be removed from office by vote of a special majority of both houses of parliament: in practice, it is very difficult to remove a sitting judge from office. This is an important fact, designed to enhance judicial independence.

Some newspaper columnists complain, from time to time, about 'unelected judges' who make decisions that the government is not happy with. This criticism (and it is always a criticism) completely overlooks the importance of judges being independent of government. The role of the judicial arm of government is to make sure that the legislative and executive arms of government do not misuse the power they have, and do not exercise powers they do not have.

For centuries, governments have tended to appoint to the bench people who (they believe, or hope) share their political and social views. There is nothing intrinsically wrong with this, so long as the new judge is also a good lawyer. But it is often the case that the new judge turns out to be so independent that their judgments dismay the government which appointed them. Remember the example of Sir Edward Coke, discussed in chapter 2. Coke was not the first, and assuredly not the last, judge who did not behave on the bench as the government had hoped.

The system of judicial appointments in Australia is very different from the system in a number of American states, where judges in many courts are elected, and stand for re-election about every five years. (It is different in the US Supreme Court, where judges are appointed for life.)

While judges in Australia are appointed to age 70, members of various quasi-judicial tribunals in Australia are appointed for a term of years by the government of the day. Their term of office may be as short as a few years. It does not take much imagination to understand that a person who holds office for a short time only, and whose re-appointment depends on the goodwill of the government, might sub-consciously favour the government's position in deciding cases in which the government is a party, or in which it has a political interest.

In the nature of things, judges' decisions do not please everyone. The losing party is generally not happy, and even the successful party sometimes thinks that they deserved more than the judge allowed them. And some successful litigants show no great appreciation of the system, because they think the result was the only possible outcome.

The tabloid press often criticise judges' sentencing decisions:

depending on the prevailing political climate, it is not unusual to see judges attacked as being out of touch with community sentiment when a convicted criminal receives a lighter sentence than the media hoped or expected.

Judges withstand these attacks — sometimes blunt personal attacks — and traditionally they say nothing. By convention, judges do not respond publicly to personal attacks on them. It is an important element of judicial independence that judges avoid entering the fray of public debate. By convention, the attorney-general of the relevant jurisdiction would speak up publicly in defence of the judiciary. Unfortunately, in recent times this convention has been overlooked, and on some recent occasions the attorney-general has either led the attack or tacitly supported it. But judges continue to observe the convention that they do not respond to public criticism.

There is a reason for the convention, and a good one at that. Judges occupy a position of special importance. They very often have to decide cases in which one side is powerful and the other side is weak. Often enough, the powerful party is the government, which is, ultimately, the employer of the judges.

It is a feature of the Australian system that courts can, and do, deliver judgments which infuriate governments, despite the fact that the judges are employed by the government.

Judges often have to decide cases in which the law is harsh and the judge has little or no discretion. A Federal Court judge once said that his oath of office required him to 'do justice according to law', but that in refugee cases he could do one or the other but not both. On 3 February 2016, the High Court of Australia gave judgment in a case that raised the question whether 267 asylum-seekers who were in Australia could lawfully be sent to Nauru. Most of them had been brought to Australia from Nauru for medical treatment. About 30 of them were babies who had been born in Australia to refugee mothers who had conceived on Nauru.

The case was decided in circumstances where there was extensive publicity about the harsh conditions in Nauru, and about the fact that asylum-seeker children on Nauru had been subjected to sexual abuse by the guards who were supposed to protect them. Various doctors who had worked in the detention centre on Nauru had said publicly that the simple fact of detention on Nauru amounted to child abuse. In short, there was a strong public view that the 267 should not be sent to Nauru.

The High Court held that they could, lawfully, be sent to Nauru.

At a public meeting soon afterwards, a law student asked: 'Would it have been better if the High Court had decided the case the other way?' At one level, the answer obviously is Yes. But at a deeper level, the question becomes: 'Should judges decide cases the way they think is best, regardless what their conscientious view of the law is?' To that question, the answer is clearly No.

When judges are asked to stretch the common law to fit new circumstances, they have much greater latitude than when they have to analyse how a statutory provision applies. The great genius of the common law is that it allowed principles to develop and adapt to new social circumstances. The modern law of negligence is a good example. Initially it helped those who were physically injured by a carelessly driven wagon, but now it extends to help those who suffer economic loss because of a carelessly prepared prospectus.

The only proper response to a law made by parliament that produces injustice is to persuade parliament to change or repeal the law.

Judges in Australia have a long and honourable record for honesty. In the 20th century, only one judge of a superior court was found to have acted corruptly. For a judge to allow his or her emotional preference to outweigh their opinion of what the law requires would be profoundly dangerous.

Quite apart from considerations of judicial purity, the problem with judges who let their personal preferences trump their understanding of the law comes into focus when a judge has a malign view of the subject matter. And, of course, social and political attitudes shift: if attitudes shift in a way that displeases the observer, he or she would be unhappy to see judicial decisions shifting in the same way.

Those in Australia (including me) who do not like some of the decisions made by some courts need to understand that we are well served by our judges: they do their conscientious best to decide cases honestly. If the law is bad, or the result seems harsh, it is generally because parliament has made bad laws. In a democracy, there can be only one response to that problem.

Legal practitioners

In Australia, a person is admitted to practice as a barrister and solicitor of the Supreme Court of their state and (thanks to mutual-recognition legislation) in each other state.

The distinction between a barrister and a solicitor is not well understood in the public mind. As a gross oversimplification, solicitors work in offices, and barristers work in courts. Of course, in practice, most barristers spend most of their time in their offices (but we call them chambers), and some solicitors go to court. For all that, barristers specialise in advocacy, whereas solicitors do many other, non-advocacy, things that most barristers understand only vaguely.

By convention, barristers practising at the independent bar in most states have to be self-employed, although this is not so all across Australia. In South Australia, Western Australia, and Tasmania, many solicitors act principally as advocates, and they form partnerships. Nevertheless, independent bars have developed in those jurisdictions, and appearance work tends to be done, increasingly, by members of the independent bar.

Not surprisingly, there are cases when a barrister knows that the client is guilty: some clients confess. What then? How does a barrister justify defending that client?

The answer lies in the way the system is designed and in the way in which the case is defended. We all know of the presumption of innocence: a person charged with an offence is presumed innocent until proven guilty beyond reasonable doubt. The reason the test of 'beyond reasonable doubt' is chosen is because it is thought, 'It is better than ten guilty people should walk free than that one innocent person should be convicted.' The presumption of innocence seems to have morphed, at least in the tabloid press, into something like a presumption of innocence except where the press think the person guilty. The presumption of innocence and the criminal burden of proof are so deeply entrenched that it is surprising to learn that the public need to be reminded of them from time to time.

In addition, the system is an adversarial one. The Crown prosecutes in order to prove the guilt of the accused. The accused is entitled to defend himself or herself, and the court must decide whether the Crown has discharged its burden of proof.

In defending a person who has told their counsel that they did the things alleged, the barrister can quite properly put the Crown to its proof. If the Crown cannot prove its case, then, according to the rules of the system, the accused is entitled to go free. This idea offends members of the public who seem willing, in the particular case, to set aside the rules of the system.

In acting for a person the barrister knows to be guilty, a barrister is simply upholding the system as it is designed. While it is not the barrister's role to judge the client's guilt, neither is it the barrister's role to change the rules of the system just because those rules may result in a guilty person going free in a particular case. That possibility is, after all, one of the assumptions on which the system is based.

Of course, the manner of the defence must be taken into account. It would be an ethical offence for a barrister to advance positive defences in circumstances where the client has confessed his or her guilt. So it would be quite improper to lead evidence suggesting that another person had fired the fatal shot or suggesting that the client was in another state at the time of the offence, if defence counsel has been told by their client that it was the client who fired the fatal shot.

4

The cab-rank rule

Two of the most important principles of the justice system are the presumption of innocence and the cab-rank rule.

Being a member of the bar involves several privileges and several restrictions. The main privilege is our right to stand up in a court and say whatever may fairly be said for a client without fear of being sued for negligence or libel. Chief among the restrictions is that we cannot form a firm or a partnership. This is to minimise the risk of conflicts of interest. That's important because of the second major restriction, namely the cab-rank rule.

The cab-rank rule is profoundly important. It is not well understood, and it is too often side-stepped. It says, in substance, that if barristers are offered a brief, marked with a fee appropriate to their skill and experience, and if they are available, they must accept the brief.[1] This is so regardless of what they think about their client or their client's cause. There is an important exception: if the barrister has a conflict of interests, he or she is not required to accept the brief. The conflict may arise from a financial or personal interest. So a barrister cannot be forced to accept a brief to prosecute his or her mother, or to act against a company in which he or she has a major financial stake; and an orthodox Jew would not be required

---

1   The cab-rank rule does not apply to solicitors. Solicitors form partnerships, and sometimes have to refuse to act for a person because one of their partners acts for a client with interests that are in conflict with those of the would-be new client of the firm.

to defend a neo-Nazi. Beyond the conflict exception, the cab-rank rule operates to ensure, as far as possible, that every client has the opportunity of briefing counsel of their choice.

The cab-rank rule is a natural corollary of the idea that it is counsel's role to advise and advocate, not to judge. All barristers have had the experience of being asked, at a dinner party: 'How can you defend a person who is so obviously guilty?' The answer is, of course, that it is not counsel's role to judge the client's guilt or innocence: that's the court's role. There are plenty of examples of clients who looked plainly guilty, but who turned out to be demonstrably innocent. Those examples, together with the presumption of innocence, should be enough to persuade the public that there is nothing ignoble about acting for a person who seems guilty or who holds unattractive views.

The rule that barristers cannot form firms or partnerships is designed to minimise the prospect of a barrister being conflicted out of acting for clients simply because one of their partners has acted against that client or is acting in a related matter. This is important because of the way the cab-rank rule works.

In recent times, the cab-rank rule came to public attention during the 2010 Victorian state election. On the first day of the election campaign, a Labor candidate was foolish enough to attack Brian Walters SC, a Greens' candidate who looked to have a pretty fair chance of being elected. The attack went along these lines: Walters was a hypocrite because he had acted for a company involved in the brown-coal industry, and in addition he had acted for Konrad Kalejs, who had been charged with war crimes arising out of his conduct during the Second World War. By acting for Kalejs, it was said that Walters was anti-Semitic. So the allegation was that it was hypocritical for Walters, a Greens' candidate, an environmentalist, and a civil libertarian, to act for the brown-coal industry and for someone alleged to have killed Jews during the Second World War.

The legal profession and the daily press reacted immediately and very sharply to the attack. *The Age* newspaper ran an editorial headed 'Labor Desperation Shows in Smear Campaign'. The editorial made the point that, 90 years earlier, a then little-known barrister called Robert Menzies argued the Engineer's Case in the High Court. In that case, Robert Menzies was arguing for a union, which might be thought to stand awkwardly with his position later as the founder of the Liberal Party. *The Age* editorialist had no difficulty in embracing the point that a barrister is not to be identified with the clients for whom he or she acts: the cab-rank rule 'ensures, among other things, that even individuals and corporations with tarnished or even repellent reputations will get legal representation: companies associated with polluting industries, for instance. Or even accused war criminals.'

The trial of Sir Roger Casement in 1916 and the trial of Stefan Kiszko in 1976 both provide useful illustrations of the importance of the cab-rank rule.

ROGER CASEMENT

The cab-rank rule was flagrantly ignored in 1916 when Sir Roger Casement stood trial in London for treason.

Sir Roger Casement had enjoyed a distinguished career in the English colonial service. He was a strong supporter of Home Rule who considered that Ireland's future could only be secured if the nationalist Irish volunteers were armed in the same way that the Ulster Volunteers were. He went to America to raise money, then to Germany. Between December 1914 and February 1915, he went to various prisoner-of-war camps in Germany and addressed the Irish prisoners, urging them to join the Irish brigade that he proposed to form. It was his speeches to Irish prisoners that constituted the overt acts of the treason with which he was later charged.

Early in the morning of 21 April 1916, Casement came ashore

at the Bay of Tralee in County Kerry on the west coast of Ireland, along with a member of the IRA and a member of the Royal Irish Rifles who had recently been released from a German POW camp.

The Easter Rising began in Dublin two days later. It was quickly suppressed, and its principal actors were summarily executed. Casement was arrested and was sent to London, where he was charged with high treason.

His trial was as politically charged as terrorist trials are today.

Before the trial began, the attorney-general, F.E. Smith, made it known that the Crown had possession of some diaries of Casement's that implicated him in profligate homosexual behaviour. These notorious 'black diaries' have since been the subject of great controversy. Smith and other members of the coalition government circulated copies of the diaries to influential people, apparently in order to dissuade them from speaking out against Casement's execution. The disgrace of Oscar Wilde was recent — still a matter of living memory. Many important figures were in fact deterred from helping Casement because of the whispering campaign that centred on the black diaries. It is fair to assume that the whispering campaign, coupled with the highly charged nature of a treason trial in the middle of a world war, was intended to dissuade fashionable counsel from accepting a brief to defend Casement: in that respect, it succeeded.

No English silk could be found to act for Casement. The brief was offered to, but was refused by, Sir John Simon KC and Gordon Hewart KC (later Lord Chief Justice).

Ultimately, Casement was represented by Sergeant A.M. Sullivan. Sullivan was silk in Ireland. He was the last of the Irish sergeants, and was initially very hesitant to accept the brief.

F.E. Smith, as attorney-general, prosecuted Casement personally. He tried to arrange for Sullivan to be given silk in England on the grounds that 'the disparity in attack and defence was too marked for a State trial'. Lord Findlay, the lord chancellor, refused his request.

It is a great pity that the trial played out this way. The case involved an interesting and important point of law, and Sergeant Sullivan was not up to the task. At the end of his final address, he said, 'My Lords, I regret to say I have completely broken down.' He then fell back into his seat and buried his head in his hands. He did not attend court the next day.

The principal question at issue in Casement's trial was the meaning of the statute under which the charge was laid. The Statute of Treasons was enacted in 1351, in the reign of Edward III. It is written in Norman French. Consistent with the conventions of the times, it has no punctuation. It defines various modes of treason. The relevant measure provides:

> Si homme leve de guerre contre notre dit Seigneur le Roi en son Roialme ou soit aherdant as enemys notre seigneur le Roi en le Roialme donant a euz eid ou confort en son Roialme ou per aillours

which translates as:

> If a man do levy war against our said Lord the King in his realm or be adherent to the enemies of our Lord the King in his realm giving to them aid and comfort in the realm or elsewhere

The only acts alleged against Casement were acts committed in Germany.

The question of interpretation can be shortly stated: is it treason to adhere outside the realm to the King's enemies? In other words, do the words *or elsewhere* qualify only the words which immediately precede them, or do they qualify the entire phrase *be adherent to the enemies of our Lord the King in his realm giving to them aid and comfort in the realm*? Put differently, if the document had been punctuated, where would the commas have been?

Sergeant Sullivan had two principal arguments: the first was based simply on the language used. The statute read more naturally as referring to adherence within the realm, and giving aid in the realm or elsewhere.

The second argument was more technical: until the 35th year of the reign of Henry VIII, no procedure existed that would have enabled a charge of adhering to the King's enemies *outside* the realm to be heard in any English court. It was unlikely that the statute had intended to create an offence for which no trial procedure existed.

The difficulty in his path was that various commentators — including Blackstone, Coke, Hale, Hawkins, and Fitzherbert — had asserted for centuries that the statute created the offence of adhering to the King's enemies outside the realm. The trial court took the same view. The motion to quash the indictment therefore failed. On the facts, which were hardly contested, Casement was convicted and sentenced to death by hanging.

(Later, as he sat in Pentonville Prison awaiting execution, Casement wrote a letter to an old friend, Richard Morten. In it, he referred to the commentators such as Blackstone and Coke: 'God deliver me, I say, from such antiquaries as these to hang a man's life on a comma, and throttle him with a semi-colon …')

On appeal, Sergeant Sullivan had a third argument. It was this: in feudal times, the barons very often held land in England and in France. In England, they owed their allegiance to the King of England. In France, they owed their allegiance to the King of France. From the time of King John, the King of England's claim to France was, to say the least, tenuous. Edward III claimed to be King of France in 1347, as did his successors down to 1801. But, in truth, feudal allegiance in France did not coincide with feudal allegiance in England. This political reality, so the argument ran, provided a rational explanation for adherence outside the realm not to constitute treason, as distinct from giving aid or comfort outside the realm.

The appeal failed.

Sergeant Sullivan had many good qualities, but he was beyond his peak when he acted for Casement. It is significant that he was refused silk in England. Given the subtlety of the arguments that were available, it is not hard to see that more skilled counsel might have got a better result. In particular, Sullivan's argument on appeal is attractively supported by logic and by history.

While it is not directly relevant to the cab-rank rule, a striking feature of the case is the conduct of F.E. Smith. He was a brilliant silk, attorney-general, and later lord chancellor. There are many famous stories about him: his hard personality coupled with his brilliance as an advocate made it inevitable that stories about him would circulate and survive.

The difficulties with Smith's role in the case can be illustrated by three things.

First, he was in the exquisitely ambiguous position of having himself helped arm the Ulster volunteers with German weapons in order to resist the implementation of Home Rule. His own conduct was in many ways similar to Casement's, although it was undertaken just before, not during, war with Germany. But many people will recognise that hypocrisy is no stranger to the law.

Second, he ran the prosecution hard: while Casement made his statement from the dock, immediately before being sentenced to death, Smith walked ostentatiously out of court. It was an act of calculated disdain for the prisoner, completely unworthy of such a distinguished member of an ancient profession.

Third, when the Court of Appeal dismissed Casement's appeal, the only remaining hope was an appeal to the House of Lords. There was great controversy in legal circles about the correctness of the judgment. An appeal to the House of Lords lay only with the *fiat* (permission) of the attorney-general — that is, with the permission of the man who had just run the trial so ruthlessly.

A delegation visited Smith in his capacity as attorney-general. They pointed out the doubts that attended the interpretation of a measure written on vellum in law French in 1351. They said that they had the support of no less a person than Sir William Holdsworth (arguably the greatest legal historian of the common law world, and author of the monumental *A History of English Law*). Smith replied archly:

> I am well acquainted with the legal attainments of Sir William Holdsworth. He was, after all, runner up to me in the Vinerian prize when we were at Oxford.

He refused his *fiat*. Casement was hanged at Pentonville prison on 3 August 1916.

It has often been said that Casement was hanged by a comma. No one with a sense of fairness could consider the result satisfactory. At the very least, it is shocking that Smith, having prosecuted the way he did, should have prevented an appeal to the House of Lords on such a novel and difficult legal question when a man's life depended on the result.

Casement was let down by a failure of the cab-rank rule.

STEFAN KISZKO

Stefan Kiszko was the son of a German mother and a Ukrainian father who had fled to England after the Second World War. They were hard-working, ordinary folk who lived in Rochdale, a metropolitan borough of Greater Manchester in north-west England. They were proud of Stefan when he got a job in the local tax office: he was the first in the family who had a job that required him to wear a suit and tie to work.

Kiszko suffered from hypogonadism — a condition in which the body doesn't produce enough testosterone. As a result, Kiszko was a large child-man: although apparently of average intelligence, he was grossly immature because of his hypogonadism. This condition was not diagnosed until he was 23.

Lesley Molseed was a small, frail 11-year-old. She lived in Rochdale with her mother and stepfather. On 5 October 1975, she agreed to go down to the shop to get some bread. Her body was found three days later, on the moors nearby. She had been stabbed 12 times. Her clothing was undisturbed, but the killer had ejaculated on her underwear.

An enormous police investigation began when the body was found. Two girls identified Stefan Kiszko as the man who had exposed himself, and the police quickly formed the view that Kiszko fitted the profile of the person likely to have killed Lesley Molseed. They pursued evidence which might incriminate him, and ignored leads that would have taken their enquiries in other directions.

THE TRIAL BEGAN on 7 July 1976. Kiszko was defended by David Waddington QC and Philip Clegg. His counsel were briefed by Legal Aid. The cab-rank rule meant, in substance, that they had no choice but to act for him, although it is hard to avoid the conclusion that their hearts were not really in the job.

On the first morning of the trial, the Crown delivered thousands of pages of additional 'unused material'. The Crown is obliged to provide to the defence a brief of all the material they will rely on at trial. In addition, they are obliged to provide material collected during the investigation on which they do not propose to rely.

The defence did not seek an adjournment. Obviously, it was impossible for defence counsel to read, much less to make strategic decisions about, such a huge quantity of material delivered at the last minute. Among the additional material was a statement by a taxi driver who admitted being the person who had (inadvertently) exposed himself in front of the two girls: this was the incident that had initially attracted police attention (wrongly) to Kiszko; it was an incident to which he had confessed in his statement to police. The taxi driver's statement gave the clearest grounds for suspecting the reliability of Kiszko's confession.

Second, the defence chose the wrong way of challenging the admissibility of Kiszko's confessional statement. A technique that is available for this purpose is called a *voir dire*. This is simply an argument in front of the trial judge, before the trial begins (or with the jury absent). Instead of seeking to exclude the confession as a preliminary matter on a *voir dire*, they sought to impeach its voluntariness and veracity in the course of the trial itself. This meant not only that the jury saw the confession, but also that they heard all of Kiszko's pitiable frailties and shortcomings as a human being.

Third, and most difficult to understand, they ran inconsistent defences. The primary defence was that Kiszko did not kill Lesley Molseed. But Kiszko had recently been put on a course of hormone treatment to deal with the consequences of his hypogonadism. The scientific evidence was that this could cause uncharacteristic changes of mood. Defence counsel put forward an exaggerated version of the likely effects of that treatment. The second line of defence was, in effect: 'He did not do it, but if he did it, it was because of the hormone treatment, which turned him into a sex monster.' It is hard to imagine how any jury could exclude the effect of the alternative defence from their consideration of the primary defence.

Kiszko appears not to have been consulted about the alternative defence. From first to last (apart from the retracted confession), Kiszko insisted that he had never met Lesley Molseed, and that he did not kill her.

It is difficult to escape the idea that his counsel did not believe in his innocence, even though Kiszko, like all defendants in a criminal trial, was presumed innocent.

He was convicted and sentenced to life imprisonment.

Kiszko's mother was the only person who clung tenaciously to a belief in his innocence. She pleaded his case to anyone who would listen. As her entreaties became more desperate and forlorn, so her audience became less receptive. But eventually, in 1987, Campbell Malone agreed to take a look at the case. He consulted Philip Clegg (who had been Waddington's junior at the trial). Clegg expressed his own doubts about the confession and the conviction. After lengthy investigations, they prepared a petition to the home secretary for access to the papers concerning the investigation and trial. Eventually, they were given access.

All the papers had been archived, and Detective Superintendent Trevor Wilkinson and his team was assigned to the job of digging through them. They discovered three vital things:

- First, the additional unused material disclosed to the defence on the first day of the trial included crucial evidence, but the late disclosure meant that the defence team did not pursue the ramifications of that evidence, which, if pursued, would have cast doubt on the reliability of the confession.
- Second, the pathologist who examined Lesley Molseed's clothing had found sperm in the semen stains on the underwear. This fact had not been disclosed to the defence or the court.
- Third, the police had taken a sample of Kiszko's semen at the time of the investigation: it contained no sperm at all, because he was medically incapable of producing sperm. This fact had not been disclosed to the defence or the court.

An innocent man had been convicted. The conviction was overturned by the Court of Appeal on 18 February 1992.

KISZKO'S CASE reveals something important about the cab-rank rule.

First, it is clear that his counsel did not believe in his defence: how else to explain the curious alternative defences noted above? But they accepted the brief nonetheless. The cab-rank rule must involve actually defending the person, however unpopular they may be.

Second, if any defence is to be meaningful, it needs to be founded on the presumption of innocence. Unfortunately, press coverage of sensational criminal trials these days makes that a difficult thing for all but the most robust advocates. The press is not shy in expressing strong views about a person accused of terrible crimes and about anyone who seeks to defend that person. Their thinking seems to go like this: *A person who commits a terrible crime is a terrible person. A person who defends a terrible person is also a terrible person.* This simple, but erroneous, logic means that barristers who honour the cab-rank rule can expect to be vilified in the popular press.

Kiszko's case also illustrates the importance of the presumption of innocence. Where a crime is peculiarly awful and a person is charged, the public seem to form a view pretty quickly that the accused person is guilty. The view will be emphatic in proportion to the horror of the crime.

As we have seen, the rationale of the presumption of innocence is that 'It is better that ten guilty people walk free than that one innocent person should be convicted.' And that same rationale underpins the requirement that the prosecution prove its case beyond reasonable doubt.

Unfortunately, the horror of a particular crime does not increase the prospects that the police will get the right person. Tabloid coverage of nasty crimes often creates the impression that the person charged is presumed guilty. And if the trial results in an acquittal, the press and the public are horrified. So much for the presumption of innocence.

There are plenty of examples of a person looking guilty, and being found guilty, but turning out to be demonstrably innocent, albeit after spending years in prison. Stefan Kiszko's case is one example.[2] There are other examples, as we are about to see.

---

2   In *Watching Brief*, I discuss Casement and Kiszko. I apologise for repeating that discussion here, but they are important cases.

5

The presumption of innocence

The presumption of innocence is central to the criminal-justice system: all people are presumed innocent until found guilty beyond reasonable doubt.

That's the theory.

In practice, the tabloid media have strong views in some cases, and they are not shy about making it plain when they think a particular defendant is guilty. And if someone is acquitted who the media think is guilty, there is an outcry in which politicians are told they must fix whatever loophole is thought to have produced the wrong result.

And it is not just the press whose views can trump those of the jury. The police often enough form a firm view about the identity of the person who committed a particular crime, and they sometimes exert themselves to achieve the result they think is right. Sometimes they do this against plain proof of the innocence of their target.

The American South has thrown up many examples of people (usually African-Americans) who have been convicted of terrible crimes, and who (after decades in gaol) are exonerated by DNA evidence that was not available at the time of their trial. Some have been exonerated that way years after being put to death. As at December 2016, defendants in 37 states had later been exonerated by DNA evidence. Since 2000, 263 people have been exonerated. They spent, on average, more than 14 years in gaol for crimes which, it was later found, they had not committed. In total, people wrongly convicted and later exonerated spent a combined total of 4,606 years in prison! The Innocence Project in the USA reveals on its website some alarming facts about the race of people convicted but later (after many years in prison) exonerated: 206 were African Americans; 104 were Caucasians; 25 were Latinos; and two were Asian Americans.

According to the Innocence Project, since 1989 tens of thousands 'prime suspects' were identified and pursued until DNA testing proved that they had been wrongly accused. They were the lucky ones: they were not convicted.

In Australia, we are not free of terrible miscarriages of justice. While it is often said facetiously that the gaols are full of innocent people (that is, people who in their own estimation are innocent), the fact remains that our system does not work perfectly.

ANDREW MALLARD

The trial, sentencing, and subsequent release of Andrew Mallard revealed significant flaws in the West Australian justice system. In particular, it demonstrated difficulties inherent in the use of circumstantial evidence and extended police interviews, particularly where the suspect was a person with a mental illness.

Pamela Lawrence had a jewellery shop in Mosman Park, an up-market suburb of Perth. On 23 May 1994, she was found murdered. She had been bludgeoned to death in her shop, in broad daylight. One hundred and thirty-six people were identified as persons of interest.

Mallard attracted police attention because he had been interviewed by the police earlier that day in relation to another matter. The police questioned him continuously for 11 hours. Though he denied any knowledge of the crime or of Pamela Lawrence, the police continued the interrogation. Eventually,

Mallard was asked by police to describe how the murder *might* have occurred — he was asked to theorise and draw the possible murder weapon. Based solely on these speculations, which the police had induced him to make, Mallard was arrested and charged with the murder of Lawrence.

He was convicted. The conviction was based on two key pieces of evidence. The first was the notes made by the police in their 11-hour interview with Mallard. According to the notes, Mallard had confessed — though this overlooked the way he had been persuaded to speculate about the way the murder had been committed. The second piece of evidence was video footage of the final 20 minutes of the police interviews, which showed Mallard's musings over how the murder might have occurred. Despite these musings being expressed hypothetically and in the third person, the police said this was his confession to the murder.

Apart from these two pieces of evidence, there was nothing linking Mallard to Lawrence or to the scene of the crime. However, Mallard did admit that he was in the vicinity of Lawrence's shop at the time of the crime: he did not see her, but was looking to buy some marijuana in Mosman Park. Mallard had no history of violence, and there was no scientific evidence linking him to the murder. In particular, there was no blood on him or any of his clothing — which was surprising, given the violent and bloody nature of Lawrence's death. Further, the prosecution could not produce any DNA evidence at trial. So Mallard's conviction was based solely on the interview notes and tapes.

Mallard was convicted of the wilful murder of Pamela Lawrence on 15 November 1995. He was sentenced to life imprisonment.

Mallard appealed. His appeal failed. He applied for special leave to appeal to the High Court. That application was refused.

The first appeal was made in 1996 to the Western Australian Supreme Court. It was quickly denied due to Mallard lacking new or fresh evidence. Next, his 1997 special-leave application to the High Court was denied. He based his request on the West Australian police's failure to record the entirety of his interview; however, it was denied, as the requirement to record interviews came into effect after Mallard's 1995 trial. Despite presenting the issue of flawed evidence to the court, his appeal was unsuccessful.

It later emerged that the prosecution had withheld relevant information from Mallard's defence team — most importantly, information about the existence of a palm print at the crime scene. It was the palm print of a previously convicted murderer, Simon Rochford.

After he had served eight years of his sentence of life imprisonment in strict security, he petitioned for clemency. The attorney-general for Western Australia referred the petition to the Court of Criminal Appeal.

Mallard's application for clemency turned on whether his speculations about how the murder may have occurred could be regarded as confessions. At the clemency hearing, more evidence came to light that the prosecution had withheld — for example, evidence that the murder weapon could not have been a wrench, as drawn by Mallard. Moreover, Mallard had said in the police interview that he had washed his clothes in salt water under the Stirling Bridge after the murder. A chemical analysis found no evidence of salinity in his clothes.

The Court of Criminal Appeal rejected the petition for clemency.

Mallard again applied for special leave to appeal to the High Court. This time, special leave was granted, and the appeal succeeded. Judgment in the High Court was given on 15 November 2005: exactly 10 years after Pamela Lawrence was murdered. Mallard had been in custody for all of that time.

The High Court held that Mallard had been wrongly convicted because crucial evidence had been withheld from the defence:

- Tests had been conducted by a forensic pathologist to determine whether wounds inflicted upon a pig's skull with a wrench were similar to the injuries suffered by Pamela

Lawrence. They weren't. The non-disclosure of this evidence was so significant that it immediately cast doubt on the accuracy of Mallard's 'confession'.

- The prosecution had removed two pages from a report that had determined the likely level of salinity in Mallard's clothing if he had washed his clothes in the river under the Stirling Bridge, as he had said in his 'confession'.
- Mallard did not fit the witness descriptions. Witnesses described a man wearing a cap (which Mallard was not) — nor he did not match witness sketches of a man with a beard and bandanna (later identified as Simon Rochford).
- Witnesses had described a man with a bandanna at times that Mallard was in the police station earlier that day in relation to another charge.
- One witness had described locking eyes with a person who was probably the murderer. Mallard was very short-sighted, which made it highly unlikely that he was the person who locked eyes with the witness.

The High Court also held that the Court of Appeal had erred in not considering evidence from a taxi driver who had driven Mallard to the area, which placed him in a different location at the time of the murder and was accordingly a credible alibi.

Additionally, the High Court was critical of the West Australian police force's decision to interview Mallard on the day he was discharged from Greylands Psychiatric Hospital.

The High Court quashed Mallard's conviction and ordered a retrial in the Western Australian Supreme Court. The West Australian police force declined to prosecute Mallard again, resulting in his release in February 2006.

Not surprisingly, the press were highly critical of the police handling of the case. A Nationwide News report included the following:

Mr Mallard, 43, this week walked free after almost 12 years behind bars. His conviction was quashed by the High Court in November because crucial evidence was withheld from the defence during his 1995 trial.

Mr Mallard's lawyers, working pro bono to exonerate him of the vicious 1994 killing, were preparing to allege a litany of police blunders at the re-trial scheduled for July. They included that:

[1] Police did not take a detailed statement, bloodied clothing or a vehicle from a person before he left the scene, contrary to accepted practice.

[2] Clothing and a blood-stained vehicle were not seized for two days.

[3] Clothing was examined by a chemist, but not by a police blood-splatter expert.

[4] Mr Mallard could not have been wearing those clothes.

[5] Evidence suggests a member of Mrs Lawrence's family was at the scene before the ambulance arrived, but evidence has never been taken from her to ascertain if she saw anything relevant to the crime.

[6] Several witnesses saw someone suspicious fitting the description of a bearded man in a bandanna, which a schoolgirl gave to police, but those leads were not followed up.

[7] People offering information about men wearing bandannas were not interviewed by investigators.

[8] Mr Mallard's lawyers have been told that bloodied items have been destroyed, as has the property book that should have recorded who ordered the destruction.

[9] The statement of a witness at the scene was not taken for three days.

[10] There was an unexplained 20 minutes on the evening of the murder in one crucial recollection of events from a person of interest.

[11] A person handled Mrs Lawrence's handbag, pointing out that her purse was missing, after being told by a constable not to touch anything.

[12] Police did not search Mrs Lawrence's house in the days after the murder to see if her purse, which was the only item allegedly stolen, was there.

[13] A large drop of blood at the foot of a copper bath, capable of cleaning a murder weapon, in a shed at the back of the shop, was never explained.

[14] A wrench allegedly used by Mr Mallard (which was proved not to be the weapon) was reported missing more than two weeks after the murder, at the same time Mr Mallard was in police custody giving an unsigned, unrecorded 'confession'.

Mallard had to fight for three years for compensation. He received partial compensation in November 2006 — $200,000, a paltry sum considering the incompetence of the prosecution and police force. He continued to fight for compensation, and was offered a 'gift' by the West Australian government — $3.25 million. He eventually accepted that amount.

A cold-case review in 2006 into the handling of the police investigation resulted in sufficient evidence being assembled to charge Simon Rochford — a previously convicted murderer whose handprint had been found at the scene — with the murder of Pamela Lawrence. It formally cleared Mallard of any wrongdoing. Rochford committed suicide in his cell in Albany Prison, Western Australia, before any trial could begin.

Five police officers were stood down over the original investigation into Pamela's murder. In addition, a 2008 Corruption and Crime Commission was established to investigate allegations of misconduct by police, prosecutors, and political figures involved in the Mallard case.

The commission report includes the following observation:

What the police, the prosecutor, and also defence counsel, failed to do was to consider the number of errors which there were in the confessional material, the number of things which Andrew Mallard simply got wrong. … the most obvious of which was his inability to identify the murder weapon. A number of police … said they never believed that the wrench was the weapon, and the pig's head testing tended to confirm this, yet no one seems to have questioned whether that fundamental mistake on Andrew Mallard's part, especially when combined with his other mistakes, did not throw doubt on the reliability of the whole confession.

The commission found numerous instances of misconduct by officers involved in the investigation and prosecution. Two of the police officers have since resigned.

FARAH JAMA

On 21 July 2008, in the Victorian County Court in Melbourne, Farah Jama was convicted of the rape of a woman who had been found unconscious in a toilet at a Doncaster nightclub. It was alleged that he had raped the woman, aged 48, in the nightclub on 15 July 2006.

The victim had entered the club at about 10.20 pm, and had been found unconscious in a toilet cubicle, locked from the inside, at about 10.50 pm. She had not drunk enough to leave her unconscious, so she asked for a full medical examination. A vaginal swab revealed traces of semen that was readily identified as belonging to Farah Jama: another woman had been swabbed the day before after a sexual encounter with Jama.

Farah Jama was 21 years old. He comes from Somalia. He told police he had never been to the nightclub where the victim was found. The victim said she had not seen or spoken to any black men in the nightclub. He was convicted and sentenced to six years' gaol.

Apart from the DNA evidence of the swab, there was no other evidence connecting Jama to the victim. As a later report noted:

> The case against Mr Jama had been mounted and pursued on the basis of a single piece of evidence; namely, the presence [of semen] on a slide and a swab, collected in the course of a forensic medical examination at the Crisis Care Unit …
>
> There was no evidence, apart from that provided by the DNA, that Mr Jama had ever attended the nightclub which was promoted as an over 28's venue and located in a suburb approximately 15 kilometres from his home. On its face, it would seem to be an unlikely place for him to go, as a young person with no known or likely cultural or other links to the area, or the venue.[1]

As it turned out, the swab taken from the victim had been contaminated, because the swab taken the day before undoubtedly had Farah Jama's semen on it. The jury paid little attention to the fact that the swab from victim's cervix showed only a minuscule amount of semen. It seems that prejudice and a desire to get a conviction did most of the work. The case of Farah Jama has been finely documented by Julie Szego in her 2014 book, *The Tainted Trial of Farah Jama*.

OTHER FAILURES OF THE PRESUMPTION OF INNOCENCE

There are other cases in Australian criminal history where innocent people have been convicted and later exonerated. In almost every case, the notoriety of the crime suggests why the police — indeed

---

1   Report by Frank Vincent AO QC, of his inquiry into the circumstances of the conviction of Farah Jama, delivered May 2010.

the entire system — felt a need to get a result, even if it turned out to be a wrong result. Most of them have been well documented, so only brief treatment is needed here.

Colin Ross

Ross was convicted in 1921 for the rape and murder of Alma Tirtschke, who was 12 years old at the time of her death. Several witnesses said Ross had confessed to them, and strands of hair, said to be from the victim, were found on a blanket at Ross's house. The strands of hair were the most compelling evidence against him. Decades after Ross was executed for the murder of Tirtschke, closer examination of the hairs found on the blanket showed, beyond doubt, that they did not come from the victim. Ross was exonerated (posthumously) in 2008.

John Button

John Button was wrongfully convicted of the manslaughter of his girlfriend, Rosemary Anderson, in Perth in 1963. He was alleged to have run her over in his car. During the police investigation, Eric Edgar Cooke confessed to killing Anderson, and disclosed facts that could only have been known to the killer. At Button's later appeal, Cooke's confession was disregarded by the court as worthless.

In 2005, Button was exonerated. He had served five years in prison for a crime he did not commit.

Darryl Beamish

Jillian Brewer was murdered in her apartment at Cottesloe, in suburban Perth, in December 1959. She was heir to the MacPherson Robertson fortune. Darryl Beamish was a deaf-mute who lived nearby and signed a confession but later withdrew it, saying it had been obtained by intimidation and threats. Eric Edgar Cooke, a serial killer, later confessed to the murder. Cooke gave evidence at Beamish's appeal, but his confession was rejected by the court, which said that the confession was 'utterly worthless' and the work of a 'palpable and unscrupulous liar'. However, shortly before he was executed for another murder, Cooke grabbed the Bible from the prison chaplain and said, 'I swear before Almighty God that I killed Anderson and Brewer.' In 2005, the Court of Appeal in Western Australia set aside Beamish's conviction. In 2011, the state of Western Australia made an *ex gratia* payment of $425,000 to Beamish. He had served 15 years in prison for a crime he did not commit.

It is worth noting that the senior counsel who championed the cause of Beamish and Button was Tom Percy QC, a highly accomplished criminal barrister who acted pro bono for both men and managed, after a long campaign, to get both of them exonerated.

Graham Stafford

Stafford was convicted in 1992 of the murder of 12-year-old Leanne Holland. Holland had been savagely mutilated and possibly tortured. She was the daughter of Stafford's former partner. On 24 December 2009, the Queensland Court of Appeal overturned Stafford's conviction and ordered a retrial. (One of the three judges thought Stafford should not be retried.) On 26 March 2010, the Queensland director of public prosecutions announced that Stafford would not be tried again. He had served 14 years in prison.

Lindy Chamberlain

So much has been written about the Lindy Chamberlain case that it is hardly worth saying anything more. Lindy Chamberlain was convicted in 1982 for the murder of her 9-week-old daughter, Azaria. Her then husband, Michael Chamberlain, was convicted as an accessory after the fact. Lindy Chamberlain said at the time that a dingo had taken her baby. Four years later, Azaria's missing matinee jacket was discovered in an area full of dingo lairs. The chief minister of the Northern Territory ordered Lindy

Chamberlain's immediate release, and the case was reopened. On 15 September 1988, the Court of Criminal Appeals of the Northern Territory overturned the convictions against both Lindy and Michael Chamberlain.

In common with other cases of wrongful convictions that have been later overturned, the conviction seems to have been the result of contestable forensic evidence and public horror at the crime: a sense that it was essential to get a conviction sooner rather than later. In the Chamberlain case, there was the added element that Lindy Chamberlain was widely thought not to have shown the right amount of grief when Azaria disappeared. In addition, the Chamberlains belonged to a religious sect that was generally regarded as too 'different' to be trusted.

-6-

Remedies

In a typical action, the plaintiff seeks various remedies. In civil litigation, the commonest remedy sought is damages. So, the plaintiff says: you behaved negligently, that caused me harm, and you should pay me damages to compensate me for the harm I suffered. If the cause of action is a breach of contract, or negligent damage to property, the measure of damage is straightforward. What amount should have been paid under the contract that was not paid? What was the cost of repairing the property? If the cause of action is personal injuries, the assessment of damages is more difficult. What amount of money will compensate a person for being blinded in one eye? What amount of money will compensate a person for being in pain for months or years?

But not all actions are about damages and financial compensation. Sometimes the plaintiff wants the legal position clarified, and asks the court to make a declaration. An example of this is the case of BWV, discussed in chapter 15, 'A right to die?'. However, a court will not make a declaration in a hypothetical case: the declaration has to be necessary for the resolution of a real legal problem.

Sometimes the plaintiff simply wants the defendant to stop behaving in a particular way. To achieve that result, the court can grant an injunction.

An injunction is an order of a court telling a person that they must not engage in a particular form of conduct, or (more rarely) that they must do certain things. So, if a person intends to build a wall that intrudes on his neighbour's land, an injunction would restrain him from trespassing on his neighbour's land. And if he has already built the wall, a mandatory injunction will require him to demolish the wall.

Injunctions are one of the most powerful devices known to our legal system.

An injunction can be part of the relief sought at the end of the case. But it is often the case that a plaintiff will seek an injunction pending the trial of the case. This is an *interlocutory injunction*: one that is granted to preserve the status quo until the court can decide who is right and who is wrong.

Interlocutory injunctions, by their nature, are granted (or not) before all the facts have been worked out at trial. Since some cases proceed on facts that are fairly clear, the court can grant an interlocutory injunction on the basis that the balance of convenience favours preserving the status quo pending trial.

INTERLOCUTORY INJUNCTIONS

In 1997, the National Gallery of Victoria was planning to hold an exhibition of works by the American photographer Andres Serrano. The exhibition was to open on 10 October 1997. The works in the show included an image of a Christian cross that appeared to be enveloped in a mist which was infused with the colours of a red-and-gold sunset. It was an interesting, even lyrical, image. The problem lay in its title: it was called *Piss Christ*.

The archbishop of the Catholic Archdiocese of Melbourne, the Most Reverend Dr George Pell, issued a writ directed to the National Gallery of Victoria seeking an injunction to prevent the exhibition of that photograph. He sought an interlocutory injunction just two days before the exhibition was due to open. Archbishop Pell relied on two major points:

(a) the exhibiting or display of an indecent or obscene figure or representation contrary to section 17(1)(b) of the *Summary Offences Act 1966*; and

(b) the common law misdemeanour of publishing a blasphemous libel by reason of the fact that the photograph is 'so offensive, scurrilous and insulting to the Christian religion that it is beyond the decent limits of legitimate difference of opinion and is calculated to outrage the feelings of sympathisers with, or believers in, the Christian religion':

The exhibition was to open on 10 October. The judge heard argument on 8 October and handed down a decision on 9 October. His reasons had to do with the foundations of aspects of our legal system.

First: is blasphemy an offence in Australian law? This raised questions about the origins of the law of blasphemy, which (ironically in the circumstances) goes back to the origins of the Church of England. When Henry VIII abandoned the Church of Rome, which did not share his views about the transience of a marriage, he established the Church of England. The Church was part of the state, and to this day the English monarch is also the head of the Church of England. Blasphemy was part of the state's way of protecting itself. Blasphemous libel was, in England, a criminal offence that protected the state by protecting the church. In Taylor's case (decided in 1727), the court said:

> Blasphemous words are not only an offence to God and religion but a crime against the law, State and government, and therefore punishable in this court or to say religion is a cheat is to dissolve all those obligations whereby the civil societies are preserved and that Christianity is parcel of the Laws of England and, therefore, to reproach the Christian religion is to speak in subversion of the law.

But this unity of church and state did not survive the journey to the Australian colonies. No Australian state has ever recognised an established church, and (since Federation) section 116 of the Australian Constitution has forbidden the Commonwealth from making any law for establishing any religion.

The second argument appears somewhat more often in interlocutory-injunction cases than the blasphemy argument. The point can be shortly stated: will the court restrain the threatened commission of an offence? If Archbishop Pell's case was well founded, the facts might have constituted an offence against section 17 of the Summary Offences Act, which made it an offence to 'exhibit or display an indecent or obscene figure or representation in a public place'.

The difficulty lay in this: it was not self-evident that showing *Piss Christ* would amount to a breach of section 17 of the Summary Offences Act. The standard of proof in civil matters (the balance of probabilities) is different from the standard of proof in criminal matters (beyond reasonable doubt). If the judge were to issue an injunction restraining the exhibition, he would be (in substance) deciding a criminal matter on the civil standard. His Honour referred to a NSW case, in which the court had said:

> [D]ifferent procedures, different rules of evidence and different rules as to the onus of proof apply in criminal and civil trials. If matters … appropriate for criminal trials could too readily be brought into courts of equity, by a claim for injunctive relief, the careful protections, developed over centuries, for the accused in the criminal trial could be put at nought …

The injunction was refused.

7

A fair go

Australians have a strong instinct for giving people a fair go, which runs in parallel with a respect for human rights. Even though Australia does not have a written bill of rights, we have a shared sense that some ideals are basic to our society. Most of the basic elements of a constitutional democracy are found in our Constitution, but others are taken for granted: we tacitly accept them as basic and inalienable. The American formulation of 'life, liberty and the pursuit of happiness' is not only familiar to us from TV documentaries: it is a pretty fair reflection of our own assumptions. For most of us, the assumption remains untested.

If we were to prepare a list of a society's shared ideals, it would include something like the right to a fair go. In 2004, the then prime minister, John Howard, reaffirmed his faith in Australia as 'a fair and decent society'. The idea that decency and fairness are woven into our way of life is so natural that we rarely question it, and so attractive that we may be reluctant to question it.

TWO PARADOXES

Certain features of our treatment of refugees stand in marked contrast to these basic assumptions. Our 'fair go' society has, through its elected representatives, inflicted extraordinary harm on a small group of innocent people. This presents two related paradoxes:

- Parliament expresses the will of the people. The Australian people are mostly decent and fair. The government is enforcing laws that are demonstrably unfair, and incompatible with ordinary notions of decency. The minority who protest at this state of affairs are disparaged as 'members of an elite'; and
- Our society, which prides itself for its respect for human rights, actively supports its government in pursuit of a policy of needless cruelty, in defiance of basic human-rights principles.

How are these things to be understood and explained? What is a citizen to do when faced with such laws?

Human rights and a just society

There is no general agreement about what constitutes a just society, although most Australians would consider that we live in one.

Genuine protection of human rights is a necessary feature of a just society. Any worthwhile human-rights framework will guarantee as inalienable rights those conditions that are generally regarded as necessary for a decent human existence. A survey of the guaranteed rights in other Western democracies shows that they all guarantee the following rights and freedoms:

1. The right to life and liberty
2. No slavery
3. No cruel or unusual punishment
4. Freedom of religion, thought, speech, press, and assembly
5. Freedom from arbitrary search and seizure
6. Due process and equal protection under law
7. The right to vote

Surprisingly few of these rights and freedoms are guaranteed by Australia's Constitution.

A denial of basic rights is not compatible with a just society. Equally, a society that denies these rights is unlikely to be a decent society, since, with few exceptions, the elements of human rights coincide with the dictates of morality. This is so even if those whose rights are denied are outsiders, not members of the society itself. A society that acknowledges the existence of human rights but accords them only to members of the polity can only maintain intellectual consistency by impliedly classifying the outsider as not really human. Erasing a person or group from the face of the human map is a moral failing of the highest order.

THE FACTS ABOUT OUR TREATMENT OF ASYLUM-SEEKERS

Asylum-seekers who arrive in Australia without prior permission are immediately detained. Until 2013, by force of the Migration Act, they had to remain in detention until they were given a visa or removed from Australia. Since 2013, most of them have been removed to Nauru or Manus Island (part of Papua New Guinea). In legal theory, they are then the responsibility of those countries, and their claims for asylum are processed by those countries.

The government, and the media, refer to boat people as 'illegals'; however, the plain fact is that there is no provision in Australian law that makes it an offence to arrive in Australia without permission and to seek asylum.[1] To the contrary, Article 14 of the Universal

---

1 On 20 February 2017, I appeared on the ABC programme *Q&A*, alongside Attorney-General Senator George Brandis. I took the opportunity to ask him whether he thought that boat people commit any offence by coming to Australia as they do. To my astonishment, he said 'Yes.' When pressed, he was not able to identify any provision which made their arrival an offence.

   He was simply wrong, but I suspect he wanted to avoid the obvious follow-up question. Why had the first Law Officer of the country not warned his ministerial colleagues that calling boat people 'illegal' was false

Declaration of Human Rights guarantees to every human being the right to seek asylum in any territory he or she can reach. Those who come here trying to exercise that right are locked up in wretched detention centres or, more recently, in remote desert islands.

Australia's system of mandatory detention has been widely criticised by humanitarian organisations, both here and overseas, and many non-government organisations (including a UN working group) have said that it constitutes arbitrary detention, thereby violating Article 9 of the International Covenant on Civil and Political Rights.

The numbers

Mandatory detention has been promoted by governments — both Liberal and Labor — as 'border protection'. It has been very popular in the electorate. For two centuries, Australians have lived in dread that we will be swamped by uninvited visitors arriving in small boats. The historical irony of this seems not to be noticed by many. This is a pity, given that the highest annual arrival-rate of people coming here uninvited, in small boats, was in 1788.

At the time of the Tampa episode, in 2001, the highest number of unauthorised arrivals in one year was just over 4,100 — most of them fleeing the Taliban or Saddam Hussein.

Despite cynical, dishonest politicians exploiting hysteria about asylum-seekers, the highest-ever annual arrival-rate of boat people was about 25,000 (in 2012). The leaders of the pack were John Howard, Philip Ruddock, Tony Abbott, and Scott Morrison.[2]

It is useful to put this in context, given the rhetoric that still

---

or misleading?

2   In 2016, Philip Ruddock was appointed Australia's first special envoy for human rights. While it is true that Ruddock had a distinguished record for upholding human rights before he became minister for immigration in John Howard's government, his appalling performance in that role, and later as attorney-general, marks him as someone who should never be let loose in any role relating to human rights.

surrounds it. Every year, 4.7 million people visit Australia, generally for short-term visits for holidays or business. Every year, between 100,000 and 200,000 people migrate permanently to live in this country. Every year — until the time of Tampa, at least — there were on average 1,000 people who arrived without authority and sought asylum; of them, more than 90 per cent were found to have proper grounds for refugee status.

The ones we lock up are not the 55,000 who overstay their visas and simply remain in the country without permission. The ones we lock up are the 1,000 or so each year, of whom more than 90 per cent turn out to be genuine refugees — already damaged and traumatised by the circumstances that bring them here.

Baxter

The Baxter detention centre, four hours north-west of Adelaide, opened in August 2002. I first visited it in early March 2004.

If you stood outside, facing east, the view was a perfect Fred Williams landscape of dull grey-green scrub on red sand, stretching away undimmed for miles to a rim of hills. If you turned and faced west, a 6-metre-high electric fence stretched away into the distance; on the other side was 20 metres of no-man's land, then another tall and glittering line of wire and mesh; inside the second fence were a series of compounds made of uncompromising corrugated iron. The compounds were so designed that the inmates had no view except of the sky; more importantly, no one outside could see those locked inside.

Baxter is no longer used as a place of immigration detention, but it is worth recalling what it was like. The fact that such a place was designed and built for this specific purpose, by a government that was increasing its popularity by mistreating refugees, is itself shocking. We could hardly have guessed that the Howard government would look relatively benign in retrospect, once Tony Abbott became prime minister.

Getting into Baxter was a long process: you had to give one week's notice, fill out a form, and show appropriate ID. You would then be escorted to an electronically controlled gate. You passed through the gate and into a metal cage. After a time — five, ten, twenty minutes — the gate at the other end of the cage would open, and you could enter a small demountable cabin; there, you would be searched and scanned. After passing through another security air-lock, you would be escorted across to the visitors' compound, where you would find the real tragedy, our hidden shame.

Asylum-seekers walked around as if still alive; they talked as if they still had a hold on rational thinking. They pressed hospitality on you: an irrepressible cultural instinct, like the unwilled twitching of a dying animal. But they were not wholly there: they were hollowed out, dried, lifeless things, washed up and stranded beyond the high-water mark. Their minds were gone: shredded, destroyed by hopelessness and despair. Children were incontinent from stress; many inmates were afflicted with blindness or lameness that had no organic origin: the bewildered mind's final, mute protest.

Mr Ruddock announced Baxter as Australia's 'family-friendly' detention centre. Presumably, that deceit was intended to distract our conscience. It was difficult to get there, so most Australians relied on the government's blandishments for their understanding of how we were treating asylum-seekers.

The consequences
The circumstances of long-term mandatory detention produce behaviour that is utterly uncharacteristic but, according to psychiatrists, utterly predictable. The detainees harm themselves, they kill themselves, they damage the environment in which they are held. Children fail to flourish, and regress into infantile behaviour. Pre-pubescent suicide and self-harm, which is almost unheard of elsewhere, is common in Australia's detention centres. Adults become

listless and depressed, or they become desperate and aggressive.[3]

Beyond all these symptoms is the dominant theme reported by a huge majority of detainees — a feeling of abject hopelessness. Whilst it would be easy to attribute this to the fact that they are denied another basic good — freedom — the fact is that these symptoms of hopelessness are rarely seen in ordinary prisons. The obvious explanation is that prisoners understand the reason for their incarceration, even though they may contest it. Refugees cannot understand why they are locked up like criminals, even though they have committed no offence. At a profound level, they rationalise their circumstances as reflecting their deep unworthiness.

Locking them up forever

In November 2003, the High Court heard argument in the case of a stateless Palestinian who had been refused a visa and, despairing of life in Woomera, had asked to be removed from Australia. The government could not remove him, because there was no country in which he had a right to live. Section 196 of the Act says that an 'unlawful non-citizen' who is detained must remain in detention until (a) they are given a visa or (b) they are removed from Australia. So: an *impasse*. The Australian government argued that, in these circumstances, it could hold the man in detention for the rest of his life. On Friday 6 August 2004, the High Court handed down judgment. By a majority of four to three, they accepted the government's argument.

A government with any moral decency would have legislated to deal with the anomaly. Instead, the Australian government argued

---

3   When I refer to Australia's detention centres, I include the detention centres on Manus and Nauru. They were established by Australia, they are funded by Australia, and they exist to satisfy Australia's refugee policies. While the Australian government prefers to say that the centres on Manus and Nauru are run by Papua New Guinea and Nauru respectively, this is nothing but a fig-leaf to cover the facts.

for the right to hold an innocent person in detention for the rest of his life.

The position put by the government reflects values incompatible with a fair and decent society; it reflects values so debased as to destroy the government's moral legitimacy. The law it has successfully defended is a bad law.

Solitary confinement

Officially, solitary confinement is not used in Australia's detention system. Officially, recalcitrant detainees are placed in the Management Unit. The truth is that the Management Unit at Baxter was solitary confinement bordering on total sensory deprivation. I have viewed a videotape of one of the Management Unit cells. It shows a cell about three-and-a-half metres square, with a mattress on the floor. There is no other furniture; the walls are bare. A doorway, with no door, leads into a tiny bathroom. The cell has no view outside; it is never dark. The occupant had nothing to read, no writing materials, no TV or radio; no company, yet no privacy, because a video camera observed and recorded everything, 24 hours a day. The detainee was kept in the cell 23-and-a-half hours a day. For half an hour a day, he was allowed into a small exercise area where he could see the sky.

Amin arrived in Australia in March 2001 with his daughter Massoumeh. She was then five years old. They were held in Curtin, and then in Baxter.

On 14 July 2003, three detention-centre guards entered Amin's room and ordered him to strip. He refused, because, apart from it being deeply humiliating for a Muslim man to be naked in front of others, his seven-year-old daughter was in the room. When he refused to strip, the guards beat him up, handcuffed him, and took him to the Management Unit.

There he stayed from 14 July until 23 July, each 24 hours relieved only by a half-hour visit from his daughter, Massoumeh. But on 23

July she did not come. It was explained to him that the manager of Baxter, Greg Wallace, had taken her shopping in Port Augusta.

The next day, 24 July, she did not arrive for her visit: the manager came and explained that Massoumeh was back in Tehran. She had been removed from Australia under cover of a lie, without giving Amin the chance to say goodbye to her.

Amin remained in detention for another eight weeks. It took three applications in court to get him released. The government did not contradict the facts, or try to explain why they had removed Massoumeh from the country: they argued simply that the court had no power to dictate how a person would be treated in detention.

The government argued that no court has power to interfere in the manner of detention. A judge disagreed, and ordered that Amin be removed from solitary confinement and be moved to a different detention centre. The government appealed.

Why the government would wish to contend for an untrammelled right to hold innocent people in solitary confinement is a mystery. I am not willing to believe that most Australians would regard these things as acceptable. Certainly, they redefine the concept of a 'fair and decent society'.

These are our taxes at work: tormenting innocent people, in ways that offend every decent instinct — and for what? To deter people-smugglers. The 2014 Human Rights and Equal Opportunity Commission report into children in detention concluded that the treatment of children in Australia's detention centres was 'cruel, inhumane and degrading', and that it constituted systematic child abuse. The minister did not seek to deny the facts or the findings: instead, she said simply that it was 'necessary', and that the alternative would 'send a green light to people smugglers'.

UNJUST LAWS

These matters are a reminder of the key fact that Jim Cairns saw so clearly 50 years ago: some laws are inherently bad. The law which requires that asylum-seekers who arrive in Australia without a visa should be detained indefinitely is an example of such a law. A law that may result in an innocent person being incarcerated for the rest of his life is an example of such a law. A law that permits the unregulated use of solitary confinement of innocent people is an example of such a law.

A society that tolerates such laws is not a just society. What is the proper response of a citizen, confronted with such laws?

Antigone

Sophocles dealt with this difficulty in *Antigone*, nearly 2,500 years ago.

Polynices has been slain. King Creon has ordered that his body remain on the hillside, where the dogs and vultures will devour it. Any person who removes the body to bury it will be put to death by stoning. Antigone is Polynices' sister. She proposes to bury his body, and captures simply the central moral point: 'He is still my brother.'

Her sister, Ismene, while sympathetic, fears doing what she knows is right. The argument is found in the following lines:

ANTIGONE: I will not urge you, no nor, if you yet should have the mind, would you be welcome as a worker with me. No: be what you will; but I will bury him: well for me to die in doing that.

I shall rest, a loved one with him I have loved, sinless in my crime; for I owe a longer allegiance to the dead than to the living: in that world I dwell forever.

But if you will, be guilty of dishonouring laws which the gods have in honour established.

ISMENE: I do them no dishonour; but to defy the State, I have no strength for that.

ANTIGONE: Such be your plea: I will go to heap the earth above the brother whom I love.

We sympathise with Antigone's instinct, and with Ismene's weakness.

Her crime is discovered, and Antigone is taken before King Creon. She explains her actions in a way familiar to those who know the natural-law theory of jurisprudence. Creon charges that she has broken the law he made, and she responds:

Yes; for it was not Zeus who made that edict; not such are the laws set among men by the justice who dwells with the gods below; nor deemed I that your decrees were of such force, that a mortal could override the unwritten and unfailing statutes of heaven. For their life is not of to-day or yesterday, but from all time, and no man knows when they were first put forth.

Not through dread of any human pride could I answer to the gods for breaking these. Die I must, I knew that well (how should I not?) even without your edicts. But if I am to die before my time, I count that a gain: for when any one lives, as I do, compassed about with evils, can there be anything but gain in death?

So for me to meet this doom is trifling grief; but if I had suffered my mother's son to lie in death a corpse unburied, that would have grieved me; for this, I am not grieved.

And if my present deeds are foolish in your sight, perhaps a foolish judge arraigns my folly.

HOPE AND EXPERIENCE

Antigone's appeal is to the natural law. Natural law is that line of legal philosophy which argues that some principles of conduct are inherent in the nature of humanity, and that a man-made law which conflicts with those basic principles is no law at all. Some things, the natural law proponents argue, are simply wrong, and human law cannot make them right. A classic example is that a parliament could decree that all people of a particular religion should be placed in concentration camps or put to death. A legal positivist would say that such a law is valid law, albeit a bad one. Natural-law theory would say it is no law at all because it seeks to authorise what is self-evidently wrong.

However, there is not much room for the operation of natural law in our legal framework. Since the late 17th century we have agreed a political structure in which the parliament is supreme. In Australia, the powers of parliament are identified by the Constitution. Laws made within the limits set by the Constitution are valid laws, no matter how harsh or immoral their operation. The courts must decide whether Acts of parliament are valid or not, and what they mean. Experience shows that they are not able to blunt bad but valid laws by reference to ordinary standards of decency.

So, the Migration Act has been held to authorise the detention of an asylum-seeker for the rest of his or her life. Likewise, the Act has been held to authorise detention in conditions of unimaginable cruelty, subject only to a theoretical right to bring an action for personal injuries.

Hence the paradoxes I started with. How does a democratically elected parliament in a decent society come to enact laws that are immoral?

In *The Quiet Revolution*, Cairns wrote:

The 'rule of law' tends to acquire some value apart from any moral ends or needs of people which it might serve. There is almost nothing in the law or elsewhere that helps anyone who thinks that law is unfair or immoral. It has come as a surprise to many Australians to know that anyone would feel he should resist a law because he thought it was *morally* bad, although they themselves resist them every day because they are a hindrance to making money or driving a car.

If wrong is being done it is a long time to wait until the next election to put it right. Even then a mandate is a very nebulous thing. Elected governments and their executives do many things the government was never elected to do, and much they do cannot ever be put right by another election. When one considers how difficult it is for the individual to have any say whatever in most things done by governments, police forces and business managements, it is not difficult to understand that direct resistance to laws and orders makes more and more sense.

...

Injustice must not be tolerated in the smallest cases or it grows and becomes a way of life. The strength of the collective, the union, the party, the State or the nation is of importance, but unless injustice to the individual is resisted, the collective can become a sordid prison.

A bill of rights

There is no doubt that, in a positivist system, a law passed by parliament within its constitutional powers is a valid law. This means that the law binds all those who are within its reach. I would prefer that the validity of a law was also contingent on its remaining consonant with basic tenets of human rights that are agreed between nations and accepted among mortals as necessary to the condition of human existence. How else to do justice despite the legal validity of the Nuremberg laws?

As we have chosen a legal-positivist model for our country, it is essential that the fundamental requirements of basic human rights are recognised within that system as limiting conditions for the validity of laws passed by parliament. In a positivist system, this can only be achieved by a bill of rights, or an equivalent instrument by whatever name.

I was, for a long time, opposed to the idea of a bill of rights. I thought the American experience suggested that a bill of rights serves mostly the interests of the rogues' gallery. This may not, of itself, be a criticism: the basic rights of the rich and powerful are rarely threatened or challenged. It is not surprising that those who are driven to assert fundamental rights are those whose position in society is modest or miserable.

But the US Bill of Rights is not the sort of thing that is intended these days when bills of rights are under debate.

A bill of rights has other problems. The record of the US Supreme Court reveals vast swings in the interpretation of the rights guaranteed to US citizens. The meaning of a bill of rights is always contestable; the contest resolves itself differently according to time and circumstances. Uncertainty in the meaning of fundamental rights can be a promise of needed flexibility or a threat of uncertainty, depending on your vantage point. And I am not yet so cynical as to think that an instrument which produces a flood of litigation is necessarily a good thing.

Judicial activism

Furthermore, the American Bill of Rights has attracted to the US Supreme Court a disproportionate amount of criticism. Any discussion of a bill of rights leads quickly to a discussion of judicial activism — a favourite target of today's conservatives. It is useful to their purposes because of its unfixed content and pejorative connotations. In a constitutional democracy, the Constitution, including a bill of rights if one has been adopted, will limit the powers of parliament. Someone has to determine whether parliament has exceeded those limits. The Constitution gives that function to the courts.

Governments do not like their power to be limited. When a judge says that parliament has gone beyond the limits set by the Constitution, frustrated governments are now inclined to attack the judges, by branding them as 'judicial activists'. This is particularly so where the limits are not obvious, or their ascertainment involves consideration of contemporary social conditions. Here, the competing considerations are clear: do the words of a Constitution have a single, fixed meaning for all time, or are they to be reinterpreted as society evolves and unforeseen social conditions emerge?

The black-letter view led to the discredited decision of the US Supreme Court in the Dred Scott case: seven of the nine justices decided that the words '… all men are created equal …' in the Declaration of Independence did not refer to African-Americans.

The alternative position was captured perfectly by Oliver Wendell Holmes. He said, 'A word is not a crystal, transparent and unchanging — it is the skin of a living thought, and changes its meaning according to the time at which, and the circumstances in which, it is used.'

Whichever view you take on the underlying question, the fact remains that the introduction of a bill of rights will almost certainly result in the ultimate appellate court being exposed to virulent criticism from all sides. This is not necessarily harmful, but if the government of the day leads the attack, there is a serious risk that the authority of the court will be weakened. The Howard government showed an unhealthy willingness to attack the courts; a federal bill of rights in Australia would very likely increase the occasion for such attacks.

Nevertheless, the past few years — in particular, the egregious mistreatment of asylum-seekers — have convinced me that Australia needs a bill of rights. Even in 1995 it would have been difficult to foresee the erosion of human rights in Australia we have seen since then. The most florid recent examples of the problem are:

- Our treatment of asylum-seekers, in particular: arbitrary detention; cruel, inhumane, and degrading treatment; the use of unregulated solitary confinement; treatment amounting to torture; the prospect of permanent detention of some asylum-seekers, even though they have committed no offence at all;
- Amendments to the security legislation permitting the incommunicado detention of people not suspected of any offence;
- The government's complacent acceptance of the detention in Guantanamo of two Australian citizens: Mamdouh Habib and David Hicks were held for years without charge and without access to independent counsel; the Australian government did nothing to help them.

These things should not be acceptable in this society. A bill of rights (by whatever name) articulates the basic assumptions on which a society is founded, and ensures that those assumptions are respected by the parliament. It can serve as an impartial benchmark of agreed values in times when the will of the majority threatens an unpopular minority.

CONCLUSION

There are two final points to be made about unjust laws that highlight the need for a bill of rights in Australia. First, the laws in question may or may not represent the views of the majority of the people. If they do, the obvious response is that mob rule does not gain legitimacy by popular acclaim. Even a democratic majority does not legitimise conduct that offends basic morality.

An alternative explanation is that the elected government achieves its political objectives under cover of deception: its laws do not in truth represent a democratic majority view, but are smuggled into the polity by lies and deception. This, in my view, is what has happened in Australia since 2001. I do not think that a majority of Australians would freely endorse the prospect of imprisoning an innocent person for life. I do not think that a majority of Australians would freely endorse the prospect of unregulated use of solitary confinement of innocent people. (If they did, it could only be by virtue of the assumption that they themselves would never be subjected to such a law.) But a group which permits others to be mistreated on condition that they themselves will not be mistreated is acting immorally, and their approval can be disregarded, at least for the purpose of moral assessment.

The Howard government consistently lied to the people of Australia, as did the Abbott government a few years later.

Howard and Ruddock lied to us by calling asylum-seekers 'illegals'; they lied about the Children Overboard affair; Mr Ruddock lied when he said the refugee-appeal system was generous, and his notorious description of Baxter as a 'family friendly' detention centre was a deception of such proportions that to call it a lie is to understate the matter.

Mr Howard's claimed adherence to Christian values is difficult to reconcile with his mistreatment of asylum-seekers. And it is very difficult to reconcile Scott Morrison's claimed Christian beliefs with his policy of brutalising asylum-seekers as a deterrent. Mr Ruddock's claimed adherence to the values of Amnesty International was a lie. The Coalition's frequent invocation of 'family values' was a lie.

In the same way, Tony Abbott's conspicuous Christianity was irreconcilable with his repeated insistence that we had to 'Stop the

Boats', even if that meant imprisoning people in hopelessness and despair in Nauru or Manus Island. And Scott Morrison — another who wore his Christian beliefs on his sleeve — lied to the public by calling boat people 'illegal', and went so far as to order departmental staff to refer to boat people as 'illegal maritime arrivals'. Ordering public servants to lie takes political dishonesty to new heights.

And then Morrison renamed his department 'Immigration and Border Protection', apparently in order to create the wholly false impression that boat people were criminals from whom we need to be protected.

When a government betrays the basic values of its people, it loses its right to govern.

Democracy depends on the honesty of governments. The parliament holds in its hands our history and our future, and it must account to us truthfully. A government which betrays that trust should be removed.

8

Legal Aid

Access to justice is an ideal warmly endorsed by politicians, but not so warmly embraced. They like the idea, but, if their conduct is any guide, they are not interested in the reality. Political enthusiasm for access to justice generally reaches its high-water mark at election time; it then recedes unless some passing crisis forces it into the public consciousness again.

Access to justice is not the same thing as access to law. The distinction is important. First, because the quality of legal assistance received may significantly affect the quality of justice delivered. Second, because what constitutes justice is, at least in some measure, subjective. A result that lawyers consider 'just' may not be seen that way by a person who, from first to last, has no understanding of the process by which the result was achieved. Third, because justice has a social dimension: if two people face a similar legal problem, and one of them has a greater prospect of a favourable result than the other, justice in the larger social sense has not been achieved.

An encounter with the court system is a daunting thing for most people. The substantive law is a jungle of complexity. Statutes are difficult to understand, and the interplay between different statutes is often unpredictable and opaque. The nature and content of the common law are mysterious to most lay people. The relationship between common law and statute is a mystery to almost everyone. Bear in mind that most people who have no legal training struggle to understand the distinction between civil and criminal law, and have no conception of administrative law. Add to all of this the laws of evidence and procedure, and it becomes a little more apparent why lawyers get to charge as much as they do.

Most lawyers will admit that, when they were undergraduates, all of this looked terribly complex, and much of it still does. It is not hard, then, to understand how daunting it is to a person with limited education, or limited skills in English. And for them, it is probably an encounter at a time of great emotional stress. Even sophisticated clients, the ones who get red-carpet treatment, have difficulty understanding the refinements of law and legal procedures. What hope for the disadvantaged? With or without help, they may understand so little of what is happening to them that, short of a perfect outcome, they may not have any sense of having experienced 'justice'.

One standard response of funding bodies is, 'Underwriting access to the law is too expensive; we cannot provide legal help to everyone.' The first proposition is probably true: law is unquestionably very expensive. Justice is expensive, but injustice is even more so.

If access to justice has any meaning, funding for Legal Aid is plainly inadequate. For practical purposes, Legal Aid is trimmed to stay within available budgetary resources.

Injustices in the area of employment can also strike with double force, because the fact of being dismissed unfairly makes it likely that the litigant will not be able to afford his or her own legal help. It is a difficult, but necessary, exercise to imagine what it must be like to be in debt, with a family to support, and to find yourself cast out of employment unlawfully but without access to legal help to take on a large, corporate employer. Few of us, as lawyers, have ever had to face such circumstances. Few of us have the ability to imagine what it is like.

Even in family law and small criminal matters, litigants go unrepresented because they cannot afford lawyers and do not qualify for Legal Aid. If they are lucky, they may get some free advice from a community legal centre.

In Australia today it is not necessarily a blessing to be an aborigine, a permanent resident with a criminal conviction, or a terror suspect. But there is another group in our society who can also fairly claim to be victims of injustice. They are not readily grouped under a convenient label as the stolen generations can be. They are that desperate group of people with valid legal rights to protect or enforce, but who abandon or compromise those rights because they cannot afford to go to lawyers and are not eligible for Legal Aid. It is a very large group.

In June 2004, the Senate Legal and Constitutional References Committee delivered its report on Legal Aid and access to justice. It is a lengthy report. In summary, it found that Legal Aid funding was inadequate to meet the need, that Community Legal Centres were inadequately funded, and that as a result there was serious injustice to vulnerable groups and an undesirably high number of unrepresented litigants. The principal findings are set out in Appendix 6. They include the following:

- The Commonwealth Priorities and Guidelines deny adequate assistance in family and civil matters;
- There is gender disparity in the distribution of Legal Aid funds in practice, resulting in indirect but significant discrimination against the circumstances and needs of women in their access to justice;
- It is imperative that there be adequate funding of legal assistance for actions taken under state/territory law involving domestic violence;
- Where violence has taken place, legal representation is needed to ensure that women can participate effectively in the legal system;
- There are overwhelming deficiencies in the Legal Aid system as it relates to Indigenous people in Australia;

- Gaps in the Legal Aid system are greatly magnified in regional, rural, and remote areas;
- Guidelines introduced in 1997 have resulted in a reduction of available legal assistance for migrants and refugees. Migrants and refugees are amongst the most disadvantaged groups in terms of access to justice;
- Improving access to justice is essential to breaking the cycle that leads to homelessness and poverty; and
- Pro bono legal help is not a substitute for an adequately funded Legal Aid system.

These are very serious findings. In practice, grants of Legal Aid are tailored to fit the available funding. The funding is inadequate. We need a system that is funded to meet the demand, rather than a system trimmed to fit the budget. Legal Aid funding needs to be increased to three or four times its present level. A substantial increase in Legal Aid funding would solve many problems for many people, and would generate a massive return in the form of increased confidence in the legal system.

A significant amount of important legal work is done, very inexpensively, by Community Legal Centres (CLCs). CLCs are independent, non-profit organisations that provide legal help to more than 350,000 people each year. They do not charge for their work. There are more than 200 CLCs in Australia, ranging in size from centres with no paid staff to centres with up to a dozen employees. In recent years, the federal government has reduced the funding to CLCs, and during its last couple of years in office had begun threatening to reduce funding further.

In July 2013, funding for CLCs was increased to about $40 million annually, but in July 2017 was reduced to about $30 million. It is worth remembering that CLCs see about 260,000 clients each year, but their funding (inadequate even before the 2017 reduction) meant that they turned away about 160,000 would-be clients each year.

It's worth thinking about the figures: $40 million a year to see 260,000 clients works out at less than $160 per client. Try that in the legal profession at large! On any view, CLCs provide an incredibly valuable and important service. Their funding needs to be increased so they can continue the work of giving ordinary Australians the possibility of access to justice.

The people who receive legal help from CLCs are generally the most disadvantaged in our society. Reducing the funding to CLCs inflicts real hardship and harm on those who can least bear it. Inadequate funding of CLCs is a direct source of great injustice in a country which still prides itself on the ideal of a fair go for everyone. The Senate enquiry report included a finding that CLCs should be properly funded to enable them to provide services that can respond to community need. The report said that the difficulties CLCs were experiencing were unacceptable. Those difficulties were a direct result of inadequate levels of funding and increased demand on CLCs, caused by restricted Legal Aid funding.

PRACTICAL CONSEQUENCES

The practical result of the present system is that only the very rich and the very poor are able to secure adequate representation in court in criminal matters and in some family-law matters. And the rest? They represent themselves or abandon their rights. The results are not happy for the courts or for the litigants. A great deal of court time is wasted as judges and magistrates try to explain the procedure to self-represented litigants. Many cases go on appeal because they miscarried at first instance. Many litigants walk away from their encounter with the legal system feeling bruised, cheated, or betrayed; feeling that they have not had justice. The dismal truth is that their perception is too often justified by the facts. Funding for Legal Aid and CLCs needs to be greatly increased.

In every court, every day, it is possible to see litigants who have to manage, as best they can, to deal with the court system. It is a daunting task. Most people cannot manage. Quite apart from the unfairness that some litigants have to face the system alone, the simple fact is that judges and magistrates find their work much more difficult when one side is not represented.

It is always a difficult thing for the public to hear lawyers asking for Legal Aid to be increased: it sounds so utterly self-interested that it is hard to take it seriously. But put that natural cynicism to one side: the lawyers who ask for Legal Aid funding to be increased are often the ones whose ordinary fee rate is vastly greater than Legal Aid pays, so they are very unlikely to be doing Legal Aid work in any event.

Every citizen of this country should try to imagine what it would be like to face a court without legal help; to be forced to abandon a good claim or defence because pursuing it is too expensive or too difficult. Don't regard all lawyers as motivated by greed and selfishness.

The health of our society is damaged each time we let someone sink to the bottom, just because we think it is too expensive to help them. For many people, Legal Aid is the only available safety net.

9

David v Goliath

Despite the cab-rank rule, the public is inclined to label barristers according to the cases they normally take. In early 1998, I was sitting in chambers when the phone rang. It was a solicitor who asked whether I would take a brief in the case that was brewing between the Maritime Union of Australia (MUA) and Patrick Stevedores. It was not the sort of work I normally did. I asked when it was likely to come on, and he said it would be in March or April. That was a problem for me: I was due to get married in March and was planning to have a honeymoon. I explained this to the solicitor and (with regret) declined the brief: I was not available. Only a barrister can fully appreciate what it is like to say 'No' to a brief. We all of us live in a state of perpetual anxiety and insecurity, and there is no guarantee that another brief will ever arrive.

When I got home that night, I told Kate what a good fellow I was: I had just said 'No' to a brief so that our honeymoon plans would not be disrupted. Her reaction was not what I had expected. She asked what the brief was about, and I explained that it was something to do with the MUA and Patrick Stevedores. She said that it was going to be a great case, and that I should ring back and say that I was available. This was not the hero's welcome I had expected. Of course, I could not ring back in order to get the brief.

I was feeling rather wounded the next day in chambers, when the phone rang again: it was another offer of a brief in the same case.

I accepted. The caller was Josh Bornstein from Maurice Blackburn. I did not know him, but he was acting for the MUA. The previous day, the call had been from a solicitor for the Victorian Farmers' Federation.

By that slight chance, I found myself acting for the Maritime Union of Australia, one of Australia's biggest and most unpopular trade unions. The case was important for other reasons, but it was interesting to see the public reaction to it and to my involvement in it. Some years afterwards, the dispute, and the case, were dramatised in a TV mini-series called *Bastard Boys*. A number of commentators in the popular press poked fun at the idea that I was portrayed in the series as a political naïf. They asserted confidently that I was a 'rusted-on leftie'. Nothing could have been further from the truth: but for my conscientious belief that a honeymoon was probably a good idea, I would have accepted the brief when it was first offered. As it turned out, I was pleased to be on the side of the union, but that is incidental.

At the time I took the brief for the MUA, I had a vague distaste for unions generally and an impression that the MUA was among the most troublesome of them. Relations between the union and Patricks had not been good for some time. Patrick Stevedores had been sprung seeking to train a group of mercenaries to stevedore ships. This operation had been carried out in Dubai, which raised suspicions and eyebrows.

Early in 1998, rumours began to circulate that Patricks were about to do something drastic. As the weeks went by, the rumours firmed into a suggestion that Patricks were about to dismiss the entire unionised workforce on the Australian waterfront. Rumours are not evidence, and so there was not much to work with.

If you had no understanding of the Workplace Relations Act, you might have wondered what would happen if Patricks acted as the rumour suggested. The answer was that the workforce would be reinstated, because of the provisions of the Act. But were there any exceptions to that? The only exception was this: if Patricks were to sell its assets and go out of the business of stevedoring, it would have no workforce to reinstate. So the next step was for us to write to Patricks asking for an undertaking that it would not dispose of its assets and not dismiss the workforce. If it did not give the undertaking sought, the refusal would provide the evidence we needed.

Courts can grant injunctions — that is, issue orders telling a party not to do certain things. There are three main sorts of injunctions: interim, interlocutory, and final. An interim injunction is one that is granted, urgently, without first giving notice to the defendant that the injunction is being sought. Typically, it orders the defendant to refrain from doing various things until the court can deal with the matter in the presence of both parties. Interim injunctions are not common: the reason for seeking an injunction without warning the other side is that you fear that they might destroy evidence in the meantime, or otherwise act so as to make it difficult or impossible to get an effective order from the court. Typically, an interim injunction is granted for only a few days, and then both parties come to court and the plaintiff seeks an interlocutory injunction.

An interlocutory injunction is an order that the defendant refrain from doing various things until the underlying action can be brought to trial (which may be many months away). Interlocutory injunctions are given without finally deciding any disputed questions of fact that will have to be decided at trial, but they have as one purpose preserving the status quo until the trial can be held and a final injunction can be granted (or withheld). For example, if the plaintiff says that the defendant threatens to bulldoze the plaintiff's house, without any right, the underlying action would be useless unless an interlocutory injunction was granted pending trial. But an interlocutory injunction will generally not be granted unless the judge thinks there is a respectable chance of the plaintiff succeeding at trial.

A final injunction will only be given after the trial of the action. It operates permanently.

The MUA wrote to Patricks, asking it to undertake not to dispose of its assets and not to sack its workforce. Patricks treated the request dismissively. Its refusal to give the undertaking was of major importance: it was hard to think of any reason why a large company with a large workforce would not give such undertakings, unless it was planning something that would have subverted such assurances. The MUA prepared a motion for interlocutory injunctions, returnable on the Wednesday before Good Friday. The motion simply sought an order restraining Patricks from disposing of its assets or sacking its workforce, pending the trial of the action.

On Wednesday morning, 8 April 1998, Australia woke to headlines saying that the entire workforce of Patrick Stevedores had been dismissed overnight, and that it had been replaced by an alternative, non-unionised workforce. When the lawyers arrived in court, counsel for Patricks announced that administrators had been appointed to Patrick Stevedores. This was a surprising turn of events. For anyone who had practised at the commercial bar in the 1970s and 1980s, it was an immediate reminder of 'Bottom of the Harbour' tax-evasion schemes. It seemed likely that the court would be unimpressed by Patricks acting precipitately and doing the very thing that the court had been asked to restrain them from doing. Moreover, they had done it while a summons to restrain them was waiting to be heard by the court.

The timing was difficult. The issues were complex and, on any view, events had unfolded in a way that could hardly have been expected. Good Friday was just two days away. The judge granted a temporary injunction, until after Easter, and directed that the matter should come back for further argument after Easter. Patricks was required to provide the MUA with all relevant documents showing what had gone on.

The picture revealed by those documents was truly astounding.

In September 1997 — six months earlier — the assets of the main stevedoring companies had been sold to new companies, and the resulting credit balances had been sent upstream to the holding company. The companies that had always employed the workforce — apparently large and successful stevedoring companies — were left with two assets only: their workforce, and contracts to provide the workforce to the new owners of the assets. These labour-hire contracts were, in effect, terminable at will by the company with the assets. The employees had no job security whatever, and no means of knowing the fact.

The effective result of this arrangement was that the labour-hire company could be jettisoned without harming the enterprise. This made it possible to dismiss the entire workforce in a single stroke. On the ground, nothing at all had changed: Patrick Stevedores still had the appearance of prosperity that it had enjoyed for many decades, but it was a mere shell. The workforce was hostage to a corporate shadow, and to a CEO with a secret plan.

The only party bound to gain from this strategy was the company that owned the assets. The only people bound to lose were the employees. As it happened, an obliging federal government had agreed in advance to provide the labour-hire company with enough cash to pay the accrued entitlements of the employees when the workforce was sacked *en masse*. Thus the risks associated with the stevedoring venture were transferred to the workers and underwritten by a government enthusiastic for waterfront reform at any price.

The case ran at an astonishing pace. The case came back before Justice North just after Easter, on 15 April 1998. The argument ran for three days. On 21 April, Justice North delivered his judgment and granted injunctions, pending a trial. At three o'clock that afternoon, the full bench of the Federal Court convened by video-link (with Justice Wilcox in Sydney, Justice Von Doussa in Adelaide, and Justice Finkelstein in Melbourne). They ordered a stay of Justice North's orders, pending an appeal.

The Full Court appeal began the next day, 22 April, and ran over to 23 April. At seven o'clock that night, the Full Court gave judgment, upholding the order of Justice North. The judgment was delivered in open court and was televised. ABC TV broadcast the judgment live to air. It was the first time that the ABC 7.00 pm news had been pushed aside. At 10.00 pm, Justice Hayne in the High Court granted a stay of the Full Court's orders, pending an application for special leave to the High Court.

In the ordinary way of things, special-leave applications in the High Court are heard by two judges, sometimes by three.

On Monday, 27 April, the High Court convened in Canberra and began hearing Patrick Stevedores' application for special leave to appeal the full Federal Court's orders. The Special Leave application was heard by all seven judges of the High Court.

The application ran until the afternoon of Thursday, 30 April. The following Tuesday, 4 May 1998, the High Court delivered judgments upholding the judgment of Justice North. The process of going from a judge at first instance, to an appeal, to a final hearing by the High Court took three weeks. Ordinarily, it would have taken between three and five years.

The case of MUA against Patrick Stevedores was a powerful example of the way the whole legal system can exert itself when a matter needs urgent attention. Of course, most litigants think their own case is terribly important, and for most litigants that is a completely reasonable assessment. But occasionally a case comes along that really needs urgent resolution. The MUA case was one of those. I had the good fortune to be on the winning side in that case. But even if I had been on the losing side, I would have been immensely impressed at the remarkable speed and agility of the court system and the way it handled a very difficult case.

It was an exciting case that significantly shifted my previous, naïve belief that governments in Australia behaved honestly. It also left me with a significantly changed view of the importance of unions. On the day that the High Court upheld the union's case, Josh Bornstein and I were approached by a member of the cleaning staff of the court who said, 'Thanks for that, fellas — we all feel a bit safer now.' Of course, Work Choices hadn't been heard of at that time. But his point was a good one: if an employer could crush the MUA, no employee in Australia was safe. Union power, responsibly exercised, redresses the imbalance of power between employers and the individual employee.

The MUA case had many dimensions, other than the legal dimension. There was a substantial battle being waged in the public arena at the same time. Regardless of the legal niceties, many Australians were shocked on the morning of 8 April 1998 when the news carried images of attack dogs and men in balaclavas taking over every major port in Australia. The immediate reaction of many was: this is un-Australian. They reacted this way despite the fact that the MUA was a deeply unpopular union, and without knowing whether any laws had been broken in the process. Regardless of the details, the whole episode seemed incompatible with the way Australians saw themselves, because it ran counter to our unconscious ideas about how Australian society works.

At the heart of the MUA case was the principle of legality — the principle that the conduct of the powerful will be tempered by the processes of law. Mediating the use of power is the hallmark of any legal system. The starting condition in any embryonic society is that might is right, but a principal purpose of government is that the legitimate interests of all — the weak and the strong — should be protected by the rule of law. That is reflected in the writing of Hobbes and Locke in the troubled 17th century. It was also a driving impulse behind the Universal Declaration of Human Rights. It is the highest aspiration of any legal system to ensure dignity and justice for all — rich and poor, powerful and weak, the popular and the despised.

While MUA and Patrick Stevedores were both relatively big and powerful litigants, behind Patricks stood the federal government, which made it unmistakably clear that it was barracking for Patricks. In some countries, that might have inclined the courts to decide the case in a way that suited the government. In the MUA and Patrick Stevedores litigation, the Australian court system responded with incredible speed, and upheld the ideals of the rule of law.

10

Petrol prices

All motorists in Australia are familiar with the petrol-price cycle: the advertised price of petrol at service stations edges downwards across the course of a week or two, and then it jumps back to where it started. Picking the right time to fill up is an engaging diversion, given that the difference between the bottom of the market and the top can be as great as 10 per cent or 15 per cent. And the need to pick the right time to fill up is compounded by the fact that, when the price at one service station jumps, so does the price at practically every other service station.

It is as if service station operators can read each other's minds. Or is it more than that?

For some time, the Australian Competition and Consumer Commission (ACCC) had been watching the petrol-price cycle in Ballarat, a regional city in Victoria with a population of around 90,000. It formed the view that various service stations in Ballarat had been coordinating their petrol prices from 1999 to 2001. The Trade Practices Act (since subsumed into the Australian Competition and Consumer Act) prohibited making or giving effect to an arrangement which had the purpose, or would have or be likely to have the effect, of substantially lessening competition. The ACCC thought that some service stations in Ballarat were parties to a price-fixing arrangement.

The ACCC has very wide powers to gather information. They got hold of telephone records of the various service stations, and they had a record of the daily price movements of petrol in Ballarat. They called in employees of the Ballarat petrol retailers to give evidence. (This procedure — the section 155 examination procedure — is a significant part of the ACCC's effectiveness. The ACCC has the power to require a person to give evidence, on oath, at the ACCC's premises for the purpose of finding out what has been going on. The interrogations are held in private, and the witnesses are prohibited from speaking to other people about what questions they were asked and what answers they gave.)

In preparation for the section 155 examinations, the ACCC had assembled all the telephone records and the petrol-price information in a special form. For each day when prices jumped, there was a set of Powerpoint slides that showed phone calls between the retailers, and the precise times of those calls. And the slides also showed when the various retailers increased their prices. Going through the slides for any given price-rise day, what emerged was a series of phone calls from retailer1 to 2 to 3 to 4, and so on, followed quickly by price rises at retailer 1, 2, 3, 4, and so on.

The retailers gave evidence during the section 155 procedure. They generally said that they knew the names of the other retailers, but never spoke to them and never had occasion to speak to them. Then they would be shown the slides. And then they made up excuses that were, for the most part, patently untrue.

They later gave evidence that they would receive a call from a competitor who would say words to the effect of, 'Take a drive down Sturt St' [one of the main streets in Ballarat], and they would understand that as meaning, 'There's a change in the market that you should know about' — meaning that the market was moving up. After the arrangement had been in place for a year or so, things became a bit less guarded. One competitor would ring another and say, 'I've had a call from (Competitor X), and he said there was a price movement going to happen at a particular time' — at times, he would even say what price it was going to.

The ACCC instituted proceedings in the Federal Court of Australia against the four companies and against four of their directors, alleging breaches of the price-fixing provisions of the Trade Practices Act. The retailers lost. The cumulative effect of the slides and their unreliable attempts to explain away all that phone contact led the court to find that they had, in fact, reached and given effect to an anti-competitive arrangement.

The court imposed fines on each of the retailers involved. For the four companies, fines totalling $13 million were imposed. For the four executives — the individuals who had been centrally involved in the contraventions — the court imposed fines totalling $400,000. (One company and its director appealed. Their circumstances were significantly different from the circumstances of the others. They succeeded on appeal.)

The Ballarat petrol-prices case took place in 2002. Since then, the petrol-price cycle has remained a conspicuous feature of the petrol market in many parts of Australia. The difficulty facing the ACCC is that any retailers who act in collusion are probably careful not to leave a trail of phone calls.

However, in 2014 the ACCC brought proceedings against some Melbourne petrol retailers, again alleging collusion. This time, the collusion was said to be by way of using an information service called Informed Sources. Retailers could subscribe to Informed Sources, and by doing so would have access to information about the pump price of petrol at all outlets of all other retailers who were also subscribers.

In essence, this gave retailers quick and efficient access to the information they would have gotten by driving around Melbourne looking at advertised pump prices: information that is conspicuously available to motorists.

ACCC sued the retailers and Informed Sources. At a mediation, the retailers and Informed Sources reached agreement with the ACCC and settled the case. But the price cycle continues.

11

Negligence

One of the most prolific and important branches of the common law is the law of negligence, which has developed over the centuries. Initially, negligence operated to impose liability for damages on (for example) the driver of a carriage who injured others by negligent driving. In 1932, the House of Lords decided a famous case called *Donoghue v Stevenson*.

The problem in *Donoghue v Stevenson* was this. On 26 August 1928, the plaintiff, Ms Donoghue, drank a bottle of ginger beer, manufactured by the defendant, Stevenson, which a friend had bought from a retailer and had given to her. The bottle was said to have contained the decomposed remains of a snail that was not noticeable until she had drunk almost the whole bottle.

She became sick, and later sued. If Ms Donoghue had bought the ginger beer herself, she could have sued the retailer for breach of contract, because the proferring of the item for sale would have contained an implied condition that the ginger beer was fit to drink. But her friend had bought the ginger beer, so Ms Donoghue did not have a claim for breach of contract.

She sued the manufacturer of the ginger beer, alleging negligence. After all, there should not have been a snail in a bottle of ginger beer, and it could only have got there by carelessness on the part of the manufacturer, since the bottle was sealed. And she was not able to inspect the contents of the bottle before the effect of the snail made her sick.

The defendant argued that, even if the facts alleged could be proved, the action could not succeed. This is a procedural step generally called a *demurrer*. It means that the underlying legal question can be resolved without the expense of a trial, on the assumption that the facts alleged would be established at trial.

The court that heard the demurrer disagreed and said the case should go to trial. That ruling was appealed. The appeal court held that, even if the facts were established, the law would not compensate the plaintiff. So it ruled that the case should be dismissed.

As can be seen from this narrative, the common law of negligence was not well developed in 1932. Today it seems unimaginable that a manufacturer of food or drink might not owe a duty of care to ensure that the goods will not injure the consumer.

Ms Donoghue appealed to the House of Lords, which was the highest court in the English legal system. (Its role has since been replaced by the UK Supreme Court.) It is worth noting, at this point, that the case went to the House of Lords on the assumption that the ginger beer was contaminated, although the facts alleged had never been tested because there had not been a trial. The appeal succeeded, whereupon the common law of negligence began an era of vigorous new growth.

It is interesting to note that the appeal succeeded by a majority of three to two. That is to say, two of the Law Lords thought that the common law did *not* impose a duty on a manufacturer to take care to avoid injuring a consumer.

Lord Buckmaster referred to the case of *Winterbottom v. Wright*, and said:

> [It] is ... an authority that is closely applicable. Owing to negligence in the construction of a carriage it broke down, and a stranger to the manufacture and sale sought to recover damages for injuries which he alleged were due to negligence in the work, and it was held that he had no cause of action either in tort or arising out of contract.

This case seems to me to show that the manufacturer of any article is not liable to a third party injured by negligent construction ...

And Lord Tomlin said:

I think that if the appellant is to succeed it must be upon the proposition that every manufacturer or repairer of any article is under a duty to every one who may thereafter legitimately use the article to exercise due care in the manufacture or repair. It is logically impossible to stop short of this point. There can be no distinction between food and any other article. Moreover, the fact that an article of food is sent out in a sealed container can have no relevancy on the question of duty; it is only a factor which may render it easier to bring negligence home to the manufacturer.

Secondly, I desire to say that in my opinion the decision in *Winterbottom v. Wright* is directly in point against the appellant.

But the most famous speech in the case was that of Lord Atkin, who was supported by Lords Thankerton and Macmillan. Lord Atkin began his speech by saying: '[T]he sole question for determination in this case is legal: Do the averments made by the pursuer in her pleading, if true, disclose a cause of action?' That is because the case had come to the House of Lords on a demurrer. He went on to say:

The rule that you are to love your neighbour becomes in law, you must not injure your neighbour; and the lawyer's question, Who is my neighbour? receives a restricted reply. You must take reasonable care to avoid acts or omissions which you can reasonably foresee would be likely to injure your neighbour. Who, then, in law is my neighbour? The answer seems to be — persons who are so closely and directly affected by my act that I ought reasonably to have them in contemplation as being so affected when I am directing my mind to the acts or omissions which are called in question ...[1]

It is probably the most quoted and best recognised proposition in the common law. And *Donoghue v Stephenson* has probably been relied on and cited in more cases than any other case in English history.

Since 1932, that simple doctrine has been held to impose liability for the careless manufacture of goods, careless medical attention, careless financial advice, and many other forms of carelessness that the House of Lords had probably not contemplated in 1932.

One of the great points of debate was whether the common law of negligence extended to cases where the damage suffered was pure financial loss, without involving personal injury or damage to property.

In *Hedley Byrne v Heller & Partners*, the House of Lords had to deal with the problem of negligent advice that resulted in pure economic loss. Hedley Byrne were advertising agents who had been asked to place advertising orders for a customer, for which they would be liable if their customer failed to pay. Before they placed the orders, they asked their bankers to look into the customer's financial position. Their bankers in turn asked Heller & Partners, who were the customer's bankers. Heller & Partners gave favourable references, but said that these were 'without responsibility'. Relying on the references, Hedley Byrne placed the advertising orders, their customer did not pay, and Hedley Byrne lost £17,000. They subsequently sued Heller & Partners for damages for negligence.

Counsel for Hedley Byrne argued, among other things:

In the present case if English law did not provide a remedy, it would be an unfortunate gap. It would be a discredit to English

---

1 *Donohue v Stephenson* [1932] AC 532. In ordinary courts, the individual decisions are called 'judgments'; in the House of Lords, 'speeches'.

law if, however fraudulent or negligent a bank might be in giving such information, there was no remedy against it. If there is no such duty as the appellants submit, it could be said successfully that the information given was either not given in writing or not under seal. But on the correct application of *Donoghue v. Stevenson* there should be judgment for the appellants.

Despite counsel's arguments, the appeal was dismissed. But it was not a complete failure. The House of Lords held that the law will imply a duty of care when someone seeking information from a party with special skill trusts him or her to exercise due care, and that party knew or ought to have known that reliance was being placed on his or her skill and judgment. But Heller & Partners had given their advice 'without responsibility', so Hedley Byrne were not entitled to rely on the advice.

Hedley Byrne v Heller & Partners is an interesting example of litigation that moves the law along but probably leaves both parties feeling wounded.

12

Class actions

*D*onoghue *v Stevenson* opened the way for injured consumers to take effective legal action against negligent manufacturers. But Ms Donoghue was lucky: the manufacturer's principal defence was that it did not owe her a duty, and on that question it went to the House of Lords. If the manufacturer had defended every aspect of the case, and had run it to trial on the facts and then through the appeals system, it is not hard to see that Ms Donoghue's resources may have been inadequate to see the battle to the end.

These days, large defendants are inclined to resist claims, and will fight them on every point if they get the chance. Given the modern imperative to maximise returns to shareholders, this is not surprising. A would-be plaintiff who has suffered modest damage because of the wrong-doing of a large manufacturer faces a difficult choice. Suppose an individual consumer has suffered a loss of $500 because of a manufacturer's negligence. Suppose, further, that thousands of others have suffered a similar loss because of the same negligence. And suppose that the cost of running a claim (to trial, then on appeal) would be $50,000 to $150,000 (this is not an unreasonable estimate, depending on the jurisdiction, and depending on the range of contested issues). An individual consumer would probably baulk at the idea of staking so much money in order to recover $500.

And it would be difficult to gather together hundreds of plaintiffs and have them all named as plaintiffs in a single action against the manufacturer — a theoretical possibility that changed in the 1990s, when Australian courts began to allow class actions to be brought.

A class action lets one person sue on behalf of all people affected by the same alleged wrong, whether or not their names are known. If the class is large, the total potential damages can be very large, even if each individual's loss is modest. The solicitors who bring class actions are allowed an increase in their permissible fees, to compensate for the fact that they have to wait until the action is finalised before they can recover most of their costs.

By this means, a wrong can be set right that would otherwise not have been sensible to litigate. Class actions provide access to justice in cases that would otherwise be uneconomic to run.

For the likely defendants, wrongful actions that would otherwise have had no financially adverse consequences for them can be sheeted home to them. Not surprisingly, the earliest class actions were resisted fiercely by the big end of town. The response of defendants in the first wave of class actions can be seen, in hindsight, as tacit acknowledegment of the fact that class actions made it possible to win compensation in cases where many individuals had suffered a wrong that caused them relatively small losses.

AN EXPLOSION

On 25 September 1998, there was a series of huge explosions at the Longford Natural Gas Plant in Gippsland, Victoria, followed by a fire. The gas plant was owned and operated by Esso. As a direct result of the explosions, Victoria's natural-gas supply stopped for a number of weeks. All home owners were without gas for weeks, and so were unable to use gas-fired appliances such as stoves and hot-water units. Many gas consumers suffered substantial property damage and consequential economic loss. Businesses that depended on gas suffered badly. A number of workers were stood down from businesses that could not keep functioning without gas.

Tens of thousands of businesses incurred losses totalling many millions of dollars.

Soon afterwards, a representative proceeding was issued in the Federal Court of Australia. It was later transferred to the Supreme Court of Victoria.

The defendants were Esso Australia Pty Ltd and Esso Australia Resources Pty Ltd. There were two plaintiffs representing the various groups who had suffered loss: business users, domestic users, and stood-down workers. Numerous third and fourth parties were joined in the proceeding. The defendants brought claims against third parties, seeking contribution: that is, they said that, if they were liable to pay any damages, then the third parties had contributed to the wrong and should contribute to the damages. The third parties brought claims against fourth parties, also seeking contribution.

The existence of so many third-party and fourth-party claims had the potential to make the trial almost unmanageable. To give some idea of the complexity of the case, there were two plaintiffs, two defendants, 26 third parties, and 24 fourth parties. The potential complexity of the case illustrates the justification for class actions: suppose a plaintiff had suffered damage because their restaurant business had closed when the gas stopped; suppose they had suffered a loss of profits amounting to $10,000. It would be a bold plaintiff who would run litigation involving two defendants, 26 third parties, and 24 fourth parties in the hope of recovering $10,000. The cost and complexity would be so great as to dissuade most litigants.

The trial judge ordered that the third- and fourth-party proceedings be heard separately from the main proceeding. This had the great advantage of preventing the main trial from becoming unworkable.

The proceeding came on for trial on 4 September 2002, and ran for about 10 weeks. The purpose of a representative action is to deal with questions of law and fact that are common to all the parties. In the Esso Longford case, there were difficult, complex questions that had to be decided. What caused the explosions? Who was responsible for the explosions? What harm was foreseeable by the person responsible? Those questions could be decided in the initial trial on liability. Obviously, the complex technical questions would be far too expensive to try at the suit of an individual plaintiff. The benefit of a class action is that the big, common questions could be decided just once and for all for those who suffered loss as a result of the explosions. The liability hearing would not decide the damages claim of each group member.

The trial judge held that the gas consumers who suffered property damage as a result of the gas stoppage were entitled to claim compensation for that damage and for any consequential economic loss. However, those who claimed purely economic loss arising from the gas stoppage failed.

Class actions first became possible in Australia in 1992, when the Federal Court of Australia was given jurisdiction to deal with them. It was a number of years before state courts were given similar jurisdiction. It took a number of years before the class-action provisions began to be used regularly: indeed, a number of commentators thought the provisions might never be used to any great extent.

The Esso case was one of the biggest and earliest class actions in Australia. The defendants, not surprisingly, adopted strategies calculated to prevent the case from achieving its objective. It is clear that the case could not have run full distance if it had been brought as an action for a single plaintiff. It was only viable as a class action. By careful case-management, the trial judge kept the matter on track, and the viability of class actions in Australia was assured.

The Esso class action was transferred into the Supreme Court of Victoria because Victoria was the first state in Australia to introduce class-action procedures into its legislation. It did that in 2000. The Victorian provisions are very similar to the Federal Court provisions.

In America, class actions have to be certified by the court as appropriate to class-action procedures. In Australia's Federal Court, and in the Victorian Supreme Court, the only requirement is that there be a 'substantial common question of fact'.

Unfortunately, some solicitors who began to run class actions were quick to identify the low-hanging fruit. In the USA, where class actions have been available for a long time, some class actions have been brought — especially in matters concerning the value of shares — that were plausible without being convincing, but which would be expensive and damaging to defend. So some defendants think it better to settle early and cheaply rather than have an action in court for years that might involve lifting the lid on the inner financial workings of the corporate defendant. This phenomenon — greenmail — which is easily recognised in America and may take hold in Australia, puts some corporate defendants in a difficult position, and brings no credit to the legal system.

13

The stolen generations

B ruce Trevorrow was born in November 1956, the illegitimate son of Joe Trevorrow and Thora Lampard. They lived at One Mile Camp, Meningie, on the Coorong. They had two other sons, Tom and George Trevorrow.

They lived at One Mile Camp because, in the 1950s, it was not lawful for an aborigine to live closer than one mile to a place of white settlement, unless he or she had a permit.

When Bruce was 13 months old, he got gastroenteritis. Joe didn't have a car capable of taking Bruce to the hospital, so some neighbours from Meningie took him to the Adelaide Children's Hospital, where he was admitted on Christmas Day 1957. Hospital records show that he was diagnosed with gastroenteritis, he was treated appropriately, and the gastro resolved within six or seven days. Seven days after that, he was given away to a white family: Mr and Mrs Davies.

The Davies lived in suburban Adelaide. They had a daughter who was about 16 at the time. She gave evidence at the eventual trial as a woman in her late middle age. She remembered the day clearly. Her mother had always wanted a second daughter. They had seen an advertisement in the local newspaper offering aboriginal babies for fostering. They went to the hospital and looked at a number of eligible babies, and saw a cute little girl with curly hair, and chose her. They took her home and, when they changed her nappy, discovered she was a boy. That's how Bruce Trevorrow came to be given away in early January 1958.

A short time later, Bruce's mother, down at One Mile Camp Meningie, wrote to the department asking how Bruce was doing and when he was coming home. The magnitude of her task should not be overlooked: pen and paper, envelope and stamp were not items readily obtained in the tin and sackcloth humpies of One Mile Camp, Meningie. But Thora managed to write her letter, and it still exists in the South Australian state archives. The reply is still in existence. It notes that Bruce is doing quite well, but that the doctors say he is not yet well enough to come home. Bruce had been given away weeks earlier.

In South Australia in the 1950s, the laws relating to fostering required that foster mothers be assessed for suitability and that the foster child and foster home be inspected regularly. Although the laws did not distinguish between white children and aboriginal children, the fact is that Bruce's foster family was never checked for suitability, and neither was he checked by the department to assess his progress. He came to the attention of the Children's Hospital again when he was three years old: he was pulling his own hair out. When he was eight or nine years old, he was seen a number of times by the Child Guidance Clinic, and was diagnosed as profoundly anxious and depressed and as having no sense of his own identity.

Nothing had been done to prepare the foster family for the challenges associated with fostering a young aboriginal child. When Bruce was 10 years old, he met Thora, his natural mother, for the first time. Although the department had previously prevented his mother from finding out where Bruce was, the law had changed in the meantime, and they could no longer prevent the mother from seeing him.

The initial meeting interested Bruce, and it was arranged that he would later go to Victor Harbour to stay with his natural family for a short holiday. When the welfare worker put him on the bus to go there, his foster mother said that she couldn't cope with him and did not want him back. His clothes and toys were posted on after him.

This time, nothing had been done to prepare Bruce or his natural family for the realities of meeting again after nine years. Things went badly. Bruce tried to walk from Victor Harbour back to Adelaide (about 80 kilometres) to find the only family he knew. He was picked up by the police, and ended up spending the next six or eight years of his life in state care. By the time he left state care at age 18, he was an alcoholic. The next 30 years of his life were characteristic of someone who is profoundly depressed and who uses alcohol as a way of shielding himself from life's realities. He had had regular bouts of unemployment and a number of convictions for low-level criminal offences. Every time he had been assessed by a psychiatrist, the diagnosis had been the same: anxiety, profound depression, no sense of identity, and no sense of belonging anywhere.

Eventually, Bruce made a legal claim that the state owed him a duty of care, which it had breached. The duty arose because the state had statutory obligations to Aboriginal children (the Aborigines Protection Board and the relevant minister had statutory duties as guardian of Aboriginal children in Bruce's position), and in addition the State of South Australia had common-law duties of care to Bruce in the factual circumstances of his case.

The trial had many striking features. One was the astonishing difference between Bruce — profoundly damaged, depressed, and broken — and his brothers, who had not been removed. They told of growing up with Joe Trevorrow, who taught them how to track and hunt, how to use plants for medicine, how to fish. He impressed on them the need for proper schooling. They spoke of growing up in physically wretched circumstances, but of being loved and valued and supported. They presented as strong, resilient, resourceful people. Their arrival to give evidence at the trial was delayed because they had been overseas attending an international meeting concerning the repatriation of indigenous remains.

The second striking feature was the fact that the government of South Australia contested every point in the case. Nothing was too small to pass unchallenged. One of their big points was to assert that removing a child from his or her parents did no harm — they even ventured to suggest that removal had been beneficial for Bruce. This contest led to one of the most significant findings in the case. Justice Gray said in his judgment:

> [885] I find that it was reasonably foreseeable that the separation
> of a 13 month old Aboriginal child from his natural mother and
> family and the placement of that child in a non-indigenous family
> for long-term fostering created real risks to the child's health. The
> State through its emanations, departments and departmental officers
> either foresaw these risks or ought to have foreseen these risks ...

That finding was not only supported by evidence; it also accords with common sense. We all have an instinct that it is harmful to children to remove them from their parents. The finding was based on extensive evidence concerning the work of John Bowlby in the early 1950s, which showed that it is intrinsically harmful to remove a child from his or her parents, in particular when this occurs after nine months of age.

At the time Bruce was given away, the Aborigines Protection Board of South Australia had already been advised by the Crown solicitor that it had no legal power to remove aboriginal children from their parents. One of the documents tendered at the trial was a letter written by the secretary of the APB in 1958. It read in part:

> Again in confidence, for some years without legal authority, the
> Board have taken charge of many aboriginal children, some are
> placed in Aboriginal Institutions, which by the way I very much

dislike, and others are placed with foster parents, all at the cost of the Board. At the present time I think there are approximately 300 children so placed ...

After a hard-fought trial, the judge found in Bruce's favour, and awarded him a total of about $800,000.

There are a few things to say about this. First, Bruce's circumstances are not unique. There are, inevitably, other aboriginal men and women who were taken in equivalent circumstances while they were children, and who suffered as a result. Although they may seek to vindicate their rights, the task becomes more difficult as each year passes: evidence degrades, witnesses die, documents disappear.

Second, litigation against a government is not for the fainthearted. Governments fight hard. It took Bruce's case eight years to get to court, and the trial ran for some months. If he had lost the case, Bruce would have been ruined by an order to pay the government's legal costs.

Judgment in Bruce Trevorrow's case was handed down in August 2007. Kevin Rudd's Labor government was elected in late 2007. The new parliament assembled in Canberra on 13 February 2008. At that first sitting, the government said 'sorry' to the stolen generations. It seemed almost too good to be true: the apology so many had waited so long to hear. And it was astonishing and uplifting to hear some of the noblest and most dignified sentiments ever uttered in that place on the hill. It is worth recalling some of the words:

> Today we honour the indigenous peoples of this land, the oldest continuing cultures in human history.
>
> We reflect on their past mistreatment.
>
> We reflect in particular on the mistreatment of those who were stolen generations — this blemished chapter in our nation's history ...

We apologise for the laws and policies of successive Parliaments and Governments that have inflicted profound grief, suffering and loss on these our fellow Australians ...

For the pain, suffering and hurt of these stolen generations, their descendants and for their families left behind, we say 'sorry'.

To the mothers and the fathers, the brothers and the sisters, for the breaking up of families and communities, we say 'sorry'.

And for the indignity and degradation thus inflicted on a proud people and a proud culture, we say 'sorry' ...

We today take this first step by acknowledging the past and laying claim to a future that embraces all Australians.

A future where this Parliament resolves that the injustices of the past must never, never happen again ...

The thirteenth of February 2008 will be remembered as a day the nation shifted, perceptibly. The apology was significant not only for marking an important step in the process of reconciling ourselves with our past: it cast a new light on the former Howard government, which had refused to apologise to the stolen generations. It set a new tone. And it reminded us of something we had lost: a sense of decency.

Most of the worst aspects of the Howard years — which lowered the bar for later governments — can be explained by the lack of decency that infected the prime minister's and his ministers' approach to government. They could not acknowledge the wrong that had been done to the stolen generations; they failed to help David Hicks when it was a moral imperative, waiting instead until his rescue became a political imperative; they never quite understood the wickedness of imprisoning children who were fleeing persecution; they abandoned ministerial responsibility; they attacked the courts scandalously but unblushingly; they argued for the right to detain innocent people for life; they introduced laws that prevent fair trials; they bribed the impoverished Republic of

Nauru to warehouse refugees for us. It seemed that they did not understand just how badly they were behaving, or perhaps they just did not care.

One of the most compelling things about the apology to the stolen generations was that it was so decent. Suddenly, a dreadful episode in our history was acknowledged for what it was. The prime minister's apology makes no difference whatever to whether or not governments face legal liability for removing aboriginal children. But it acknowledged for the first time that a great moral wrong was done, and it acknowledged the damage which that caused. The most elementary instinct for justice tells us that when harm is inflicted by acts that are morally wrong, there is a moral, if not a legal, responsibility to answer for the damage caused. To acknowledge the wrong and the damage and to deny compensation is simply unjust.

From that point on, events can play out in a couple of different ways. One possibility is that members of the stolen generations will bring legal proceedings in various jurisdictions. Those proceedings would occupy lawyers and courts for years, and would run according to the circumstances of the case and the accident of which state or territory was involved. The worst outcome would be that some plaintiffs would end up the way Lorna Cubillo and Peter Gunner ended up a few years earlier: crushed and humiliated. Or they might succeed, as Bruce Trevorrow did. Either way, it would be a very expensive exercise for the state, and a gruelling experience for the plaintiff.

A second possibility is that a national compensation scheme could be established, run by the states, territories, and the Commonwealth in co-operation. The scheme I advocate would allow people to register their claim to be members of the stolen generations. If that claim was, on its face, correct, they would be entitled to receive copies of all relevant government records. A panel would then assess which of the following categories best described the claimant:

a) removed for demonstrably good welfare reasons;
b) removed with the informed consent of the parents;
c) removed without welfare justification, but survived and flourished;
d) removed without welfare justification, but did not flourish.

The first and second categories might receive nominal or no compensation. The third category should receive modest compensation — say, $5,000–$25,000, depending on circumstances. The fourth category should receive substantial compensation — between, say, $25,000 to $75,000, depending on circumstances.

The process could be simple, co-operative, and lawyer-free, and could run in a way consistent with its benevolent objectives.

If only the governments of Australia could see their way clear to implementing a scheme like this, the original owners of this land would receive real justice in compensation for one of the most wretched chapters in our history.

Until such a scheme is introduced, members of the stolen generations will have good reason to think that they have been denied justice.

14

Not seeing the wood for the trees

Gunns Ltd was established in 1875. It is Australia's largest integrated hardwood and softwood forest-products company.

In 2004, Gunns' logging operations were coming under increasing attack from environmental groups. Apparently, Gunns found those attacks irritating. On 13 December 2004, it filed a writ against 17 individuals (including Greens senator Bob Brown) and three corporate entities: the Wilderness Society, the Huon Valley Environment Centre, and Doctors for Native Forests. The writ was accompanied by a 216-page Statement of Claim comprising more than 500 paragraphs. It claimed damages (including aggravated and exemplary damages), injunctions, and costs for disruption of the plaintiff's businesses allegedly caused by the defendants.

An average Statement of Claim might run to 10 or 20 pages; in earlier times, a claim was more likely to be just a few pages long. For anyone experienced in litigation, a Statement of Claim that runs to 216 pages seems extravagant: all 20 defendants were startled to see how bloated the claim was. It identified nine different 'actions' in which various of the defendants were said to have been involved from time to time. These were given evocative names, including the Lucaston Action, the Triabunna Action, the Styx Action, the Burnie Action, the Japanese Customer Action, and the Banks Action.

These 'actions' were alleged to have been part of a 'Campaign Against Gunns'. Details of the campaign were said to be found in paragraphs 14 to 525 of the Statement of Claim.

Some defendants were alleged to have been involved in just one or two of the alleged 'actions'. No defendant was alleged to have been involved in every 'action'. All the defendants foreshadowed that they would seek to strike out the Statement of Claim. Then, shortly before the strike-out application was to be heard, Gunns produced a proposed Amended Statement of Claim. In it, there was a significant increase in the number of allegations of fact with respect to the cases on conspiracy, especially with respect to the logging-disruption campaigns. There was also a change in the way in which the plaintiff sought to combine all of the individual tortious claims into the 'Campaign against Gunns'. The defendants resisted Gunns' application to file the Amended Statement of Claim, which was 150 pages longer than the original, and just as complex.

The judge who heard Gunns' application noted that 'the function of a statement of claim is to set out with sufficient clarity the case which the defendant must meet ...' He said in his ruling:

> Although in respect of each of the forest actions named, defendants have specific allegations of tortious conduct made against them, because of the various allegations of agency in amended statement of claim (including in the introductory paragraphs to which reference has already been made) and the extensive and confusing cross-referencing used in substantive paragraphs and particulars, it would be extremely difficult, if not impossible, for any particular defendant to determine with certainty whether he or she was alleged to be liable for any particular act of tortious conduct in respect of any particular forest action. One has only to embark upon the exercise of trying to ascertain exactly what is alleged against any particular defendant to rapidly come to the realisation that not only is the exercise an extremely frustrating and barren one, but it is also one not likely to lead to a certain conclusion. Thus, the pleading fails its fundamental purpose of informing each of the defendants of the case he, she or it has to meet.

The judge refused Gunns' application to file the proposed Amended Statement of Claim. He said:

> The criticisms made of the amended statement of claim in this ruling are by no means all those that could have been made. As the pleading will not be permitted to be placed on or remain on the record, it would be a singularly unprofitable exercise to attempt to describe every defect in it which needs correction …

In August 2005 (eight months after it had first issued proceedings), Gunns sought to file a third version of its Statement of Claim. Version 3 was 221 pages long, and ran to 714 paragraphs. The judge struck it out.

Gunns eventually broke its case into smaller components, discontinued its action against some defendants, and finally settled against all defendants. It did not recover damages or costs from anyone. It paid the costs of some defendants.

Whether Gunns regarded its litigation strategy as successful is less clear. The defendants had achieved a series of wins against it. On the other hand, Gunns had succeeded in locking a number of defendants in litigation for years: the last parts of the action finally settled about five years after the litigation started. It is all too easy (for lawyers especially) to overlook how stressful litigation is for individuals, especially individuals for whom losing a case might mean financial ruin. It is not hard to imagine that the board of Gunns might have been told that the litigation had at least kept the defendants off the barricades for a long time.

Most people who have been litigants would agree that litigation is not a game for the faint-hearted — especially so when the contest is one of David and Goliath, where a large, well-resourced company sues an individual who can never hope to match the financial strength of the other side.

Despite our best endeavours, there are times when our justice system seems to embody the theory of justice outlined by the Athenians to the Melians: the strong do what they can, and the weak suffer what they must.

15

A right to die?

In 1992, a woman who, for the purposes of the later litigation, was called BWV was diagnosed with Pick's disease. Pick's is a rare neurodegenerative disease that causes progressive destruction of nerve cells in the brain. Symptoms include dementia and loss of language.

In 1995, she had a percutaneous endoscopic gastrostomy (PEG) tube inserted into her abdomen. The PEG provided her with nutrition and hydration, because by 1995 she was incapable of eating or drinking.

In late 1999, she could no longer be managed by her family at home, and was admitted to a nursing home.

In February 2003, at the request of BWV's husband, the Public Advocate was appointed limited guardian of BWV, with the power (and the duty) to make decisions concerning her medical treatment. Later in 2003, the Public Advocate applied for court permission to have the PEG tube withdrawn. The consequence of withdrawal was that BWV would die.

At the time of the Public Advocate's application, BWV was doubly incontinent; she was receiving regular pressure care; she would be moved into a shower by a hoist; and she was receiving medications, as well as nutrition and hydration, through the PEG. She had not appeared conscious, or to have any cortical activity, for approximately three years. She appeared to have no cognitive capacity at all and had no bodily functions, other than those which were reflexes. She appeared to have no conscious perception of input from any of her sensory pathways.

Although her brain stem continued to function normally, the medical evidence was that the damage to her cortex was irreparable. There was no prospect of any recovery, or improvement of any kind in her condition.

Furthermore, the medical evidence was that the nutrition, hydration, and medication delivered via the PEG tube served no purpose other than keeping her alive.

The *Medical Treatment Act 1988* (Victoria) allows a guardian, on behalf of a patient, to refuse medical treatment. The medical evidence was that provision of nutrition and hydration via a PEG was 'medical treatment' within the meaning of that term in the Act. The Act did not permit a guardian to refuse palliative care on behalf of a patient, but the doctors said that the provision of nutrition and hydration via a PEG did not constitute palliative care.

The Public Advocate's application, then, was simply this: Can I withdraw the PEG so that BWV will die? It is difficult to imagine a more fraught application, or a more fraught decision for a judge to make.

When BWV began to show the first signs of Pick's disease, she and her husband had discussed what they would want if either of them was in a condition of such helplessness. He said they had '… always said if anything like this happens, do something about it. I remember it clearly. We promised each other that we would do something about it'. Easy to understand; easy to say. Not so easy to do.

One of BWV's daughters said, 'I feel very certain that what my dad has said is what she would have wanted. They had a very excellent relationship. I feel absolutely certain that she would not want to live under these circumstances …'

The Medical Treatment Act includes a number of definitions, including these:

'medical treatment' means the carrying out of -

    (a) an operation; or

    (b) the administration of a drug or other like substance; or

    (c) any other medical procedure -

    but does not include palliative care;

'palliative care' includes -

    (a) the provision of reasonable medical procedures for the relief of pain, suffering and discomfort; or

    (b) the reasonable provision of food and water; ...

The purposes of the Act are identified as 'to clarify and give legal effect to the right of a patient to refuse unwanted medical treatment'; and 'to enable an agent (including a guardian) to make a decision about medical treatment on behalf of an incompetent patient'.

The Act seeks to grapple with an old, but increasingly important, problem: when can a patient say that he or she is done with life and wants no more treatment; and when can someone make that decision on their behalf, in circumstances where the patient is no longer capable of formulating, or communicating, their wishes?

The trial judge, Morris J, referred to an English decision, in which Lord Justice Hoffmann said:

[T]he sanctity of life is only one of a cluster of ethical principles which we apply to decisions about how we should live. Another is respect for the individual human being and in particular for his right to choose how he should live his own life. We call this individual autonomy or the right of self-determination. And another principle, closely connected, is respect for the dignity of the individual human being: our belief that quite irrespective of what the person concerned may think about it, it is wrong for someone to be humiliated or treated without respect for his value as a person.[1]

---

1   *Gardner re BWV* [2003] VSC 173 at [42]'.

Morris J approached the matter in a similar way. He said:

> In my opinion, the intent of parliament in excluding the provision
> of food and water from the concept of medical treatment was to
> ensure that a dying person would have food and water available
> for oral consumption, if the person wished to consume such
> food or water. It can hardly have been the parliament's intention
> that dying patients would be forced to consume food and water.
> Further, in my opinion, the extension of the concept to artificial
> nutrition and hydration would produce odd results, contrary to the
> purpose of the legislation to allow patients, or agents or guardians
> on their behalf, to choose to refuse medical treatment and to die
> with dignity.[2]

The judge decided that the Public Advocate had the legal power
to have the PEG tube removed. He held that the provision of
nutrition and hydration via a PEG to BWV constituted medical
treatment within the meaning of the Act, and that the refusal of
further nutrition and hydration, administered via a PEG, to BWV
constituted refusal of medical treatment, rather than refusal of
palliative care.[3]

As a result, the PEG tube was withdrawn, and BWV slowly died.

It is worth wondering whether this is the right way to deal with a
problem that is bound to become increasingly common in the West.
Ordinary considerations of human dignity and decency suggest that
inducing a quick and painless death would be, in an indefinable
way, more ... humane. A long time ago, Arthur Clough (1819–
1861), in his poem 'The Latest Decalogue', caught the problem well:

> Thou shalt not kill; but need'st not strive
> Officiously to keep alive

---

2 *Gardner re BWV* [2003] VSC 173 at [82].
3 *Gardner re BWV* [2003] VSC 173 (29 May 2003).

People are living longer than ever before. An increasing number of people slip into dementia, either because of their great age or because of Alzheimer's disease or similar conditions. In the USA, there are more than 5 million people who have been diagnosed with Alzheimer's. The disease is now rated as the sixth-commonest cause of death in the USA, and for people over 65 it is the fifth-commonest cause. In the three years from 2013 to 2016, deaths from Alzheimer's in the USA increased by more than 70 per cent. Research suggests that, starting at age 65, the risk of developing the disease doubles every five years. By age 85, between 25 per cent and 50 per cent of people will exhibit signs of Alzheimer's disease.

The picture in Australia is no more cheerful. Dementia (including dementia caused by Alzheimer's) is the second leading cause of death in Australia, and there is no cure.

Worldwide, there are more than 46 million people with dementia, and the number is expected to increase to 131 million by 2050, which represents an increase of about 5 per cent per year.

Many people in the West who have lived rich and fortunate lives would be appalled by the possibility of living (possibly for years) with no cognitive faculties and no memories: in short, living lives that are a contradiction of everything their life stood for before dementia hit.

The decision in BWV was right, in my opinion. But the practical outcome of the decision was awful, even if it was all the law allowed. Some people hold the view that human life is so sacred that no person can take it away. Other people hold the view that a person's life is their own to suffer it or to end it as they choose. I'm with the second group. Science has perfected ways to end a human life painlessly and in dignity. For many years, Dr Rodney Syme has been a powerful advocate in Australia for this approach.

If governments genuinely regard a dignified human life as a goal to be honoured, they should make end-of-life decisions broader and more accessible. Of course, it is necessary to make sure that end-of-life decisions genuinely reflect the thinking of the person who is most directly concerned, and it is important to guard against opportunistic manipulation by those who might prefer an early, rather than a delayed, inheritance.

What needs to be avoided is the political hypocrisy that claims to value human dignity but is willing to watch human beings die slowly, miserably, as a shadow of the person they once were, and in circumstances against which they have protested while capable of expressing their views.

In short: voluntary euthanasia is rational and decent. It should be legal, so long as it *is* voluntary.

16

Suspected terrorists?

Scott Parkin is an American peace activist. Wikipedia describes him as a 'peace, environmental and global justice organizer, community college history instructor, and a founding member of the Houston Global Awareness Collective. He has been a vocal critic of the American invasion of Iraq, and of corporations such as Exxonmobil and Halliburton. Since 2006, he has worked as a campaigner for the Rainforest Action Network, organizing campaigns against Bank of America, Citibank, TXU and the Keystone XL Pipeline. He also organizes with Rising Tide North America.'

In June 2005, Scott Parkin came to Australia on a six-month tourist visa. While in Australia, he engaged in political-protest activities, and, unbeknownst to him, ASIO prepared an adverse security assessment concerning him.

On 8 September 2005, ASIO provided the security assessment to the Immigration Department. The department immediately cancelled his tourist visa. As a result, Parkin became a non-citizen without a visa. By virtue of section 198 of the Migration Act, he was detained, and was to be held in detention until he had a visa (which seemed unlikely) or until he was removed from Australia. On 10 September, officers of the Department of Immigration took Parkin into immigration detention and held him there. On 17 September, officers of the department removed Parkin from Australia and returned him to the USA.

To add insult to injury, on 14 September, the Department

of Immigration gave Parkin a notice requiring him to pay the Commonwealth of Australia $11,688.34 for the cost of his detention and removal.

Parkin later said, 'I was pretty baffled as to why I was locked up.' His bafflement was increased when the director-general of ASIO told a Senate committee that Parkin had not been violent while in Australia. But he said it was information about Parkin's behaviour in Australia that led to the adverse assessment.

Parkin called for ASIO to make the adverse security assessment public. He said:

> I'd like them to open up the assessment and see what they have about me in there that led them to this conclusion, so I can at least defend myself. Other than in ASIO, no one has come forward to say I advocated violence in any of the training. There was never a time I advocated violence or disruption of any sort, other than spirited protest.

Parkin was concerned that, unless he was able to clear his name, it would be difficult for him to return to Australia. He brought proceedings in the Federal Court of Australia seeking, in effect, for ASIO to disclose the basis on which it had made an adverse security assessment of him.

At the same time as Parkin's case was proceeding through the Federal Court, the Australian government's Pacific Solution (version 1) had been brought to an end. Most of the people held on Nauru had been assessed as refugees. Nauru did not have the resources (or the will) to keep them there indefinitely. John Howard's government bowed to the inevitable, and brought the refugees from Nauru to Australia.

All but two of them.

Two Iraqi men, Mohammad Hassan and Muhammad Farouq (not their real names), had been assessed as refugees but had lately been adversely assessed by ASIO. As a result of the adverse assessments, they would not be given visas to come back to Australia. (I say 'back to Australia' because, like all the other refugees warehoused on Nauru, they had first arrived in Australian territory seeking a safe place to live, but had been taken to Nauru against their will by the Australian government.)

So here we had three men — Parkin, Hassan, and Farouq — whose futures had been blighted by an adverse assessment from ASIO. None of them knew why they had been adversely assessed; no one would tell them why they had been adversely assessed; none of them had broken any law. So the question was: can a government instrumentality make a decision that will grossly affect a person's future, in circumstances where that person is unable to find out what test has been applied, by whom, and what supposed facts have been taken into account?

Hassan and Farouq issued an action to be heard in parallel with Parkin's — action in the Federal Court, challenging the right of ASIO to make adverse security assessments without giving the affected person an opportunity to know the facts on which the assessment was based.

There is a principle of administrative law that an administrative decision-maker must afford natural justice. The content of 'natural justice' varies according to circumstances. Did natural justice require ASIO to allow Parkin, Hassan, and Farouq to know the test that was applied, and the facts to which that test was applied, so as to afford them some opportunity of defending themselves against the likely consequences of an adverse assessment?

Hassan and Farouq complained that no facts existed which would justify an adverse assessment by ASIO; that ASIO had taken account of irrelevant matters, namely supposed facts which were not facts, and had failed to take account of the true facts. In addition, they complained that ASIO had failed to give them an opportunity to answer, explain, or contradict any fact or circumstance it intended to take into account in preparing the adverse assessment.

By the time the matters came on for hearing in 2010, Scott Parkin had dropped out of the legal action.

The interviews with ASIO had been unsatisfactory. Hassan had written to the director-general of ASIO, as follows:

> My name is Mohammed Hassan, ID nr05-0009, 29 years old, Iraqi pending case on Nauru. I would like to write about the abusive way that I have been treated during the interviews of the security assessment by the officials of this Dept.
>
> In November 2004, there were some officials from the Aus government on Nauru and called for the Iraqi nationals to be interviewed. My turn was in the first day when they began the interviewing. ... (They) started asking me about my background and I replied to his questions frankly, openly and honestly. The interview took 2 hours.
>
> 3 or 4 days later, I was told by IOM that that officer would interview me again. During that interview, the officer ... had uncivilized manner in conducting the interview. He used to put me under severe mental pressure. He hit me with his fist on my knee. He had been screaming most of the time of the interview. ...
>
> During this interview I had felt that I am sitting down before officials from a Saddam's regime security organization.
>
> On the 24th of January this year I was called to be interviewed. When I arrived to Topside location I found the same officer ... is present there. He told me that all of what I have told him in the previous interviews is not true, and that I have to change what I have said and to say the truth. I strongly rejected that accusation and told him that I have told nothing but the truth and I have nothing to add or to change. He told me that if I changed my statement, then he will grant me a visa to Aus because he is the one who can do so. ...
>
> On the 11th of April, I was told by [XYZ] that he has been told

by those officers that I had not been cooperative in the interviews. And now I am wondering how I haven't been cooperative after all that unbelievable way in treatment and that I have been waiting for my refugee determination for over than 7 months.

I am also wondering why those officers didn't mention that I haven't been cooperative earlier. Why they waited four months to tell this. I feel it as a psychological war. And they waited all this time just to put me under mental pressure.

Thank you for you giving time to read my letter.

He did not get any proper response.

The idea of spending years more on Nauru — the possibility of being held in detention for the rest of their lives — was too much for Farouq. He had a nervous breakdown. Mental-health facilities on Nauru are virtually non-existent. So Australia took Farouq from Nauru to Brisbane, where he was placed in a mental hospital.

In the meantime, both Hassan and Farouq began their legal action against ASIO in the Federal Court of Australia. The essential points of their claim were these:

- Since September 2002, they had been held in Nauru.
- In September 2005, they were assessed by Australia as refugees.
- Subsequently, ASIO had adversely assessed them.
- As a result of the ASIO assessment, they had not been given visas to enter Australia.
- No facts existed that would justify the adverse assessments;
- ASIO took account of things that were untrue;
- ASIO failed to take account of the true facts;
- ASIO failed to afford natural justice in that:
  - it failed to tell them of any facts on which it proposed to rely in making the adverse assessment; and
  - it failed to give them an opportunity to answer, explain

or contradict any facts it intended to take into account in preparing the adverse assessment.

Before the case came to trial, ASIO revised its assessment of Farouq, who was still in a mental hospital in Brisbane. It decided that he should not be adversely assessed. As a result, he was given a protection visa.

Hassan's witness statement included this passage:

> The biggest issue that was raised repeatedly in my interviews with ASIO was that of my father's profession. As mentioned at the beginning, the head of the religious organisation that my father worked for was the Grand Ayatollah Sayed Mohammad Sadeq al-Sadr. My father was reasonably close to the Grand Ayatollah and was in almost daily contact with him by virtue of his role within the organisations. The Grand Ayatollah was, and his three sons were, once invited to by my father to our home.
>
> The Grand Ayatollah's third son is Muqtada al-Sadr. That time was the only time I time I saw Muqtada al-Sadr face to face which was a very brief moment no longer than 30 seconds of greeting. I did not have any contact with anyone in Iraq after I left [in May 1997] and neither did my family to the best of my knowledge. The Grand Ayatollah and his two other sons were assassinated in 1999.

Both Hassan and Farouq said in their witness statements that they had never in their lives been involved in espionage, sabotage, politically motivated violence, promotion of communal violence, attacks on Australia's defence system, or acts of foreign interference, and that they had never in their lives done anything which could be understood as any of those things.

The things they listed were the matters on which an adverse assessment may legitimately be based.

This evidence was not challenged, and yet the trial judge

dismissed the application. His judgment included the following observations:

> [T]he applicants were forced to rely on their personal evidence that they had not done anything which would warrant the making of an adverse security assessment about them and on the failure of the Director-General to gainsay this evidence by himself leading evidence as to the reasons why he had made the adverse security assessments. The Director-General sought to meet these contentions by submitting that he could not place such evidence before the Court without infringing the public interest immunity which had been found by the Court to apply to such information.
>
> ...
>
> In the present case the Director-General's reasons for making the adverse assessments are not known. For reasons which I have given, it was not open to him to expose his reasons to scrutiny. In these circumstances neither the general denials proffered by the applicants nor the Director-General's failure to disclose his reasons permit the inference to be drawn that no facts existed which supported the judgment to which the Director-General came in each case.
>
> ...
>
> The applicants [must demonstrate] that the Director-General [took irrelevant matters into account]. In the absence of published reasons this required them to establish a basis for drawing the necessary inferences. The Director-General was under no obligation to demonstrate, by way of evidence or inference, that he had not had regard to irrelevant considerations...

In short: Hassan and Farouq were obliged to demonstrate that ASIO had acted on wrong grounds, but they were not allowed to know the grounds it had acted on, so they failed.

Australia persuaded Sweden to consider taking Hassan. After a one-hour interview with him, Sweden accepted Hassan, and he has lived in that country since about 2008.

The Senate Legal and Constitutional Legislation Committee held an enquiry into the provisions of the Migration Amendment (Designated Unauthorised Arrivals) Bill 2006. It delivered its report in June 2006. The report included these paragraphs:

> The most telling example of the consequences of Australia forcing refugees to be assessed outside any legally enforceable framework is the plight of the two men still stuck on Nauru after more than 4 and a half years — [Mohammad Hassan], now aged 29, and [Muhammad Farouq], aged 26. Even though they have both been found to be refugees, they have received an adverse security assessment from ASIO which they are unable to appeal or have reviewed. They are unable to even find out what the adverse security assessments are based on.
>
> Neither I nor anyone else is able to comment on whether this ASIO assessment is justifiable. However, given the serious and fundamental flaws involved in some of the refugee assessments by DIMIA officials ... it is not unreasonable to suggest that mistakes of fact or reasoning may have been made in the ASIO assessment.

It is a disturbing idea that a person's life and liberty can be so profoundly affected by a faceless official, operating in complete secrecy and beyond the reach of effective judicial scrutiny. That is the stuff of a police state.

AFFORDING NATURAL JUSTICE to people who come into contact with the bureaucracy is an assumption on which our system is founded. It is an aspect of fair treatment. National security is also self-evidently important, so how can the requirements of natural justice be balanced against the interests of national security?

Imagine: ASIO is considering making an adverse assessment of a person, and it has gathered information about him. Natural justice might suggest that the person must be given a chance to comment on the information: after all, it may be wrong, or biased, or it may be capable of being explained away innocently by reference to other information known only to the person being assessed. On the other hand, showing the person the information may indirectly disclose the sources; it might even disclose that a member of the person's family or inner circle is an ASIO informant … It is easy to imagine ways in which the dictates of natural justice might be inconsistent with national security.

In the case of Hassan and Farouq, the court found that, because it did not know what facts ASIO had taken into account, it could not make a judgment that there were no facts which supported the decision.

So, the result is that a person's life can be irrevocably blighted by a government instrumentality, and the person affected will not be allowed to know why, or on what facts, or on what reasoning. In such cases, ASIO is a law unto itself.

This brings to mind an important decision of the UK House of Lords. The UK parliament had passed an Act which provided that a refugee in Britain who was also a suspected terrorist could be put in detention for up to 12 months 'to preserve the life of the Nation'. The point was that, as a refugee, the person could not be sent back to their country of origin because that would involve Britain in a direct breach of its obligations under the Refugees Convention. And detaining a person who had not been charged or convicted of any offence could not be squared with the Human Rights Act. The Human Rights Act reflects the European Charter of Human Rights, and it is a condition of membership of the European Union that the member states have domestic laws which reflect the

European Charter. But there is a get-out: a law can be passed that is inconsistent with the Human Rights Act if that law is necessary 'to preserve the life of the Nation'.

So the question for the House of Lords was whether the particular law was valid. In an 8:1 decision, the House of Lords determined that the laws did not comply with the UK Human Rights Act. Lord Hoffmann said:

> [T]he real threat to the life of the nation, in the sense of a people living in accordance with its tradition laws and political values, comes not from terrorism but from laws such as these.

This is a powerful idea. In Australia, we have been persuaded by politicians that we live at great risk, and that, to protect us from that risk, we need harsh laws. It all looks OK as long as those laws never have an impact on your life. But if you live at the margins — if you are a refugee, or an Aborigine, or a Muslim, or you are homeless, or a possible security risk, or suffering from a mental disability — those laws look dangerous. And they can operate dangerously.

It is worth remembering the observation of a leading politician, spoken many years ago:

> [T]he people can always be brought to the bidding of the leaders. That is easy. All you have to do is tell them they are being attacked, and denounce the pacifists for lack of patriotism and exposing the country to danger. It works the same way in any country.

Those words were spoken by Hermann Goering in April 1946, in an interview in his cell during his trial at Nuremberg.

All of us should remember Lord Hoffmann's comment set out above. And in connection with it, we should bear in mind the famous (and better-known) comment of Jack Lang, later paraphrased by

Paul Keating: 'Always back the horse named self-interest, son. It'll be the only one trying.'

Although it is always tempting to pursue our own immediate self-interest, it is easy to forget that our interests in the long term may be better served by protecting someone else's interests in the short term. Preserving the fundamental values of our society is profoundly important, even if it comes at an inconvenient cost.

Of course, it may be politically popular to reduce tax rates, even if that means reducing support for those at the margins; but we value a society that protects the weak and disadvantaged.

And for those of us who do not live at the margins, it is useful to recall the famous observation of Martin Niemöller, which is set out on page 226.

17

Hate mail

When I did the Tampa case in August 2001, I received death threats. Although I had acted in some fairly contentious cases before (including Alan Bond's, the cash-for-comment enquiry, and the waterfront case of Patrick Stevedores against the Maritime Union of Australia), the Tampa case was the first one that attracted death threats.

But that case had opened my eyes to what Australia was doing to refugees. It worried me. I recognised fairly soon that the courts had a very limited ability to soften a very harsh policy. I concluded that speaking out publicly might shift the public attitude, and if the public attitude shifted far enough, the politics would follow.

As I became increasingly vocal as a campaigner against the mistreatment of asylum-seekers, I started getting hate mail. Whenever I spoke publicly about the subject, which was quite often, I would get hate mail. And that is a fascinating experience for a polite, conservative, middle-class lawyer. When I say hate mail, I mean mostly emails, but also actual letters: letters that came written in closely spaced paragraphs, the full page, then up the side of the page and over to the back, and usually in strange, scrawly writing — you know what I mean. The people who write actual letters are a very forgetful bunch: they never remember to put their name and address on the letter, so it was not possible to reply to them.

But with email you can always reply to them, even if you don't know who they are, and most of the hate mail came as email.

And they were awfully rude. They questioned my sincerity, my motives, my integrity, my intelligence, my parentage … they were astoundingly, unremittingly rude. Still, I decided — consistent with my theory that it was going to be necessary to change the mind of the public — that here was a group who were putting their hand up saying, *I disagree with you*. So I decided to answer them all.

I had not done the maths. I had not worked out how long it would take. It did take a while, but I made a point of answering every single email. Typically, they would fall into a few observable patterns. I would sit up late at night writing, in substance:

> Dear so and so. Thanks for your email. I gather you don't agree with me. But did you realise they haven't broken the law, and they come in small numbers, and we lock them up indefinitely, and so on.

And, in most cases, that triggered a response from them. Every single response was polite — going from flaming and furious and capitals and everything, to room-temperature polite, in a single step. And some of them would say, *Gosh I didn't realise that. OK. Fair enough. I agree with you.* And others would say, *Look that's all very interesting. I didn't realise that, but* … and then the 'but' would be a disguised way of saying, *They are Muslims*, or *They are different from us*, or *I don't like them*, or *There's something wrong with them*. So I'd write back saying, 'Thank you for getting back to me, but did you know there is this, that, and the other?' I gave them the facts.

This went on for about four or five years. At the end of it, I estimate that more than half of the people who wrote these screaming emails ended up saying, in substance, *Thank you for discussing this with me. I agree with you now*. About 25 per cent ended up saying, in substance, *Thank you for discussing this with me. I don't agree with you, but I think it's good you stand up for what you believe in*. And the rest …? I had better not say.

This is all by way of explaining that after each of the next two chapters of this book I am including some (anonymised) samples of hate mail I received.

I should add that it all ended quite well. The hate mail had petered out by about 2005 or so. The issue had gone off the radar. The boats had pretty much stopped coming, and things were OK. But out of the blue, in late 2007, I was checking my email and I noticed a bit of hate mail. I wouldn't say I had missed getting hate mail, but I was eager to see what this one said. It read as follows:

> Dear fuckwit.
> What makes you think that being a QC means anyone is interested
> in your opinions. Why don't you fuck off and die.

Engaging intellectually with this was quite a challenge. I thought his principal position was probably right, unless it was a judge who wrote it, but I did not think it was. And so, rather than concede the ground, I used a line a friend had given me. I wrote back, saying:

> Dear —
> Thank you for your email. The offer of your sister is interesting.
> Please send photographs.

Even now, it gives me a warm glow to remember that. I imagined his face exploding and his hair falling out. But he replied. He said:

> Fair enough. I suppose I was a bit over the top.

It occurred to me that there was a rational mind there after all. So I wrote back to him, saying, in substance, *Look, I don't mind. It's OK, but you know I've been talking about this stuff for quite a while. Why did you write just now? Did it all get too much for you? Or did you just stumble on it?*

And he wrote back, saying:

I should come clean. I'd had a huge night out. I met a bloke I couldn't stand. We were arguing about refugees. I should have written to him I suppose. Instead I wrote to you. Actually I think you are doing a pretty good job, so please ignore me.

Every cloud has a silver lining.

(When boat people became an issue again in 2012, most people who wanted to express their disagreement with me did it on social media. Generally speaking, a piece of abuse squeezed into 140 characters lacks the interest or literary merit of an abusive email.)

18

Human rights

Human rights arise from the fact of being human. The distinction is clearer when regard is had to the legal treatment of other creatures. We acknowledge the existence of other species, and the law protects them to some extent. But we recognise a difference of kind between human beings and the rest of the sentient world. To give some simple examples, the laws of all civilised nations recognise a qualitative difference between killing a human and killing an animal; they recognise a qualitative difference between stealing property, however valuable, and kidnapping a person. It is the quality of humanness, then, that carries with it a set of unique considerations; in a civilised society, these considerations are ultimately formulated as rights.

The origin of recognisable human-rights discourse can be found in the second half of the 18th century. Tom Paine published *The Rights of Man* (and was prosecuted for sedition); the American colonies declared their independence from Britain; the French rose up against the aristocracy.

In 1776, the American colonists signed the Declaration of Independence. Its opening words are as memorable as they are noble:

> We hold these truths to be self-evident, that all men are created equal, that they are endowed by their Creator with certain unalienable Rights, that among these are Life, Liberty and the pursuit of Happiness.

The French Revolution proclaimed the ideals of 'Liberty, Equality and Fraternity'.

However, the record of human rights is stained with hypocrisy. High ideals are voiced and approved, but they are frequently not matched by performance.

The ideals of the French Revolution were not evident in the Terror that settled in blood the accounts of ages. One hundred years later, Captain Dreyfus was prosecuted for alleged espionage, but the prosecution was a monstrous fraud, driven by the deeply ingrained anti-Semitism in the army and the Church.

And 100 years after the Declaration of Independence, the US Supreme Court had to interpret the words of the preamble, in a suit brought by Dred Scott. He was a slave, but he had lived for 13 years in a non-slave state. Relying on English precedents, he sued for a declaration that he was a free citizen of the United States. The court held, by a 7:2 majority, that the words 'all men are created equal' did not refer to African Americans. The language of the judgment is shocking to modern ears:

> The question before us is whether (African American slaves) compose a portion of this people, and are constituent members of this sovereignty? *We think they are not, and that they are not included, and were not intended to be included, under the word 'citizens' in the Constitution*, and can therefore claim none of the rights and privileges which that instrument provides for … citizens of the United States. On the contrary, *they were at that time considered as a subordinate and inferior class of beings* who had been subjugated by the dominant race, and, whether emancipated or not, yet remained subject to their authority …
>
> They had for more than a century before been *regarded as beings of an inferior order, and altogether unfit to associate with the white race* either in social or political relations, and so far inferior that they had no rights which the white man was bound to respect

… (they were) bought and sold, and treated as an ordinary article of merchandise and traffic whenever a profit could be made by it. (*emphasis added*)

THE 20TH CENTURY

In 1945, the Allied forces mounted the world's first prosecution of war criminals. Europe lay shattered, and the world held its breath in horror as the first films of Belsen concentration camp were made public. In his closing address at the first Nuremberg trial, Robert Jackson, chief prosecutor for the US, said:

It is common to think of our own time as standing at the apex of civilization, from which the deficiencies of preceding ages may patronizingly be viewed in the light of what is assumed to be 'progress'. The reality is that in the long perspective of history the present century will not hold an admirable position, unless its second half is to redeem its first.

In the aftermath of World War II, it looked as though the second half of the 20th century might, indeed, redeem the first. In 1948, the Universal Declaration of Human Rights (the UDHR) set the style for human-rights thinking. Its prefatory words set the tone:

Whereas recognition of the inherent dignity and of the equal and inalienable rights of all members of the human family is the foundation of freedom, justice and peace in the world,

Whereas disregard and contempt for human rights have resulted in barbarous acts which have outraged the conscience of mankind, and the advent of a world in which human beings shall enjoy freedom of speech and belief and freedom from fear and want has been proclaimed as the highest aspiration of the common people,

Whereas it is essential, if man is not to be compelled to have recourse, as a last resort, to rebellion against tyranny and oppression, that human rights should be protected by the rule of law ...

The declaration articulated, in high prose, the essential values of a dignified humanity. Subsequently, the International Covenant on Civil and Political Rights embodied as binding commitments most of the ideals of the UDHR. It makes great promises. Its signatories — almost every country in the world — promised each other to secure for their citizens the essentials of a decent human existence.

But the fine rhetoric did not prevent the subsequent genocide in Rwanda, or the terrible ethnic cleansing in former Yugoslavia. It was powerless to prevent the stain of Apartheid in South Africa, the widespread disappearances and torture in Chile arranged by General Pinochet, or the killing fields of Pol Pot's Cambodia.

And while the resounding phrases of the UDHR were being crafted and polished, America was making a secret deal with Japanese war criminals. These men, doctors and scientists, had run the notorious Unit 731 in Harbin. There they performed medical experiments on untold thousands of Chinese civilians. These experiments, including vivisection of pregnant women, were as bad as anything done by Mengele in Auschwitz, but they are less well known: the Americans granted the scientists immunity from prosecution in exchange for their research results.

HUMAN-RIGHTS PROTECTION IN AUSTRALIA

Unlike other Western democracies, Australia has no coherent human-rights protection. Our Constitution says nothing about human rights, although it contains section 116, which prevents the Commonwealth from legislating in respect of religion. In addition, the division of our Constitution into chapters (including chapters creating the three arms of government: legislature, executive, judiciary) was early on held to imply a separation of powers of those arms of government. Unlikely though it may seem, the separation-of-powers doctrine has had a profound effect on Australia's constitutional development.

In addition, various implied freedoms and rights have been found in our Constitution, including freedom of political discussion.

There have been a few times in Australia's recent history when a bill of rights was proposed or considered. In 1956, the ALP Joint Committee on Constitutional Review supported a stronger rights protection. In 1969, the ALP national conference supported entrenchment of fundamental civil rights and liberties. In 1974, Lionel Murphy introduced the Human Rights Bill, which lapsed after the 1974 double dissolution. In 1985, Lionel Bowen introduced a Human Rights Bill, but it was blocked in the Senate. In 1988, there was a human-rights referendum, which attracted only 31 per cent support and was defeated. In 2007, the ALP policy platform was amended such that there would be an enquiry into the statutory protection of human rights. After Kevin Rudd became prime minister, the National Human Rights Consultation Committee was established, with Frank Brennan as its chair. The committee began in November 2008 and delivered a report in September 2009, recommending a federal Human Rights Act. But in April 2010, Kevin Rudd announced, peremptorily, that he would not introduce a Human Rights Bill.

It is important to notice that the Brennan committee was only asked to enquire into a statutory bill of rights. Of course, amending the Constitution is difficult, as was apparent in 1988, and it is easy to find pragmatic arguments for not even attempting to introduce a constitutional bill of rights. But a statutory bill of rights can be repealed, altered, or over-ridden just as easily as any other statute, so it can offer only fragile protection.

Victoria and the Australian Capital Territory both have statutory bills of rights. The ACT has the *Human Rights Act 2004*. Victoria has the *Charter of Human Rights and Responsibilities Act 2006*.

THE ARGUMENT IN AUSTRALIA ABOUT
A BILL OF RIGHTS

At the 2020 Summit in Canberra in April 2008, a view emerged strongly that Australia should have a federal bill of rights. That call — fairly predictable in the circumstances — triggered a series of public speeches and papers as Cardinal Pell, Bob Carr, and others raised their voices against such a Bill.

These pre-emptive strikes against the possibility of a federal bill of rights had one thing in common: they did not identify what sort of bill they were opposed to.

Some of their criticisms might have been valid if the proposal was for a US-style bill. But, so far as I am aware, no one in Australia was pushing for a US-style bill of rights. The US bill is an 18th-century document with its roots in 17th-century England, and with a dash of Magna Carta providing the best bits.

Modern bills of rights do not concern themselves with the right to bear arms or the quartering of soldiers. They are concerned instead with the sort of rights recognised by the Universal Declaration of Human Rights: equality before the law; the right to life; protection from torture and cruel inhuman or degrading treatment; freedom from forced work; freedom of movement, privacy, and reputation; freedom of thought, conscience, religion, and belief; freedom of expression, of peaceful assembly, and of association; protection of families and children; humane treatment when deprived of liberty, and so on.

WHAT ARE WE TALKING ABOUT?

To make the debate about a bill of rights intelligible, it is useful to identify what we are talking about. Because we are not talking about a US-style bill of rights, some people prefer to speak of a charter of rights in order to make the distinction plain: that was the approach in Victoria. Nevertheless, it is worth bearing in mind that there is no magic in the name: a charter of rights and a bill of rights are the same thing; the US Bill of Rights is quite different. As discussed in chapter two, the US Bill of Rights is an 18th-century document with almost nothing in common with modern bills of rights. The rights protected by a modern bill of rights are — broadly speaking — the sort of rights addressed in the Universal Declaration of Human Rights that Australia adopted in 1948.

It would be difficult to find any serious disagreement about the nature of those rights — freedom from arbitrary detention, freedom from torture, freedom of thought and belief, equality before the law etc. The disagreement arises when the means of protecting those rights is in issue.

Broadly speaking, a modern bill of rights can be a weak model or a strong one; and it can be an ordinary statute or constitutionally entrenched. The arguments for and against a bill of rights change profoundly according to the model under discussion. Unfortunately, conservative commentators never identify exactly what it is they are condemning.

Statutory bills of rights can be disregarded or repealed if the parliament so wishes. A constitutional bill of rights, on the other hand, cannot be repealed or altered except by referendum. A Constitution (in theory) expresses the will of the people directly, and binds the parliament. A statute, by contrast, expresses the will of the people indirectly through their elected representatives and can be made, changed, or repealed by the parliament.

A strong model charter creates rights of action: if a person's rights are breached, he or she may be able to sue for damages. A strong model may also forbid parliament to do certain things and thereby directly limit the power of the parliament.

A weak model simply requires parliament to take protected rights into account when passing legislation. If the people's representatives wish to disregard those rights, they must say so plainly. This means that the parliament will be politically accountable if it decides to disregard rights which it has previously resolved to respect. In addition, it guides judges in the way they should interpret legislation, so as to preserve rights rather than defeat them.

The ACT and Victoria both have statutory, weak charters of rights. So long as the public and the conservative commentators find it alarming to protect rights, a weak statutory model is a good solution.

It is usual to see a range of arguments put up against the adoption of a bill of rights. The standard ones are as follows:

- Human rights cannot be created: they derive from moral truths;
- Our rights are adequately protected by the majesty of the common law;
- It is anti-democratic because it would transfer power from parliament to unelected, unrepresentative judges;
- It would transfer power disproportionately to minorities;
- It would not work; and
- It would be a lawyers' feast.

Let me deal with each of these in turn.

'Human rights cannot be created.'
An interesting, but uncommon, argument is that human rights cannot be created by a parliamentary act: they derive from moral truth. Moral truth is a product of natural law. Aristotle (384–322

BC) is said to be the father of natural law. If that is true, Thomas Aquinas was its tutor. It provided the bedrock of the common law in England, it informed the writing of Hobbes and Locke, and it is reflected in the preamble to the US Declaration of Independence:

> When in the Course of human events, it becomes necessary for one people to dissolve the political bands which have connected them with another, and to assume among the powers of the earth, the separate and equal station to which the Laws of Nature and of Nature's God entitle them, a decent respect to the opinions of mankind requires that they should declare the causes which impel them to the separation.--We hold these truths to be self-evident, that all men are created equal, that they are endowed by their Creator with certain unalienable Rights, that among these are Life, Liberty and the pursuit of Happiness.--That to secure these rights, Governments are instituted among Men, deriving their just powers from the consent of the governed,--That whenever any Form of Government becomes destructive of these ends, it is the Right of the People to alter or to abolish it, and to institute new Government, laying its foundation on such principles and organizing its powers in such form, as to them shall seem most likely to effect their Safety and Happiness. ...

Sophocles' play *Antigone*, which I discuss on pages 106–7, turns on a conflict between natural law and legal positivism. (Sophocles lived from 496 BC to 406 BC. *Antigone* was written in about 442 BC, well before Aristotle was born.)

Today, Antigone would be convicted. An appeal to natural law does not work. Legal positivism has displaced natural law. Laws made by parliament are valid laws, subject to constitutional constraints. That is the consequence of the violent constitutional struggles of the 17th century, coupled with the unsympathetic clarity of a written Constitution.

A right that is not recognised by law is nothing but a pious hope. If rights are to be any use at all, they must be recognised in law. Increasingly, this means that they must be recognised in an act of parliament.

'Our rights are already protected.'
Within the scope of its legislative competence, parliament's power is unlimited. The classic example of this is one given earlier: if parliament has the power to make laws with respect to children, it could validly pass a law that required all blue-eyed babies to be killed at birth. The law, although terrible, would be valid. One response to this is that a democratic system allows that government to be thrown out at the next election. This is not much comfort for the blue-eyed babies born in the meantime. And even this democratic correction may not be enough: if blue-eyed people are an unpopular minority, the majority may prefer to return the government to power. The Nuremberg laws of Germany in the 1930s were horrifying, but were constitutionally valid laws that attracted the support of many Germans.

Generally, parliament's powers are defined by reference to subject matter. Within a head of power, parliament can do pretty much what it likes. Thus, as we have seen, the Commonwealth's power to make laws with respect to immigration has in fact been interpreted by the High Court as justifying a law that permits an innocent person to be held in immigration detention for life, where he is liable for the daily cost of his own detention. (The detainee's statutory liability for the cost of detention has since been repealed.)

The question then is this: should we have some mechanism that prevents parliaments from making laws which are unjust, or which offend basic values, even if those laws are otherwise within the scope of parliament's powers? If such a mechanism is thought useful, it is likely to be called a bill of rights, or a charter of rights, or something similar.

In November 2003, two cases were heard together by the High Court of Australia. Together, they tested key aspects of the system of mandatory detention. One was the case of Mr al-Kateb.[1] He had arrived in Australia as a boat person, and had sought asylum. He was placed in immigration detention because the Migration Act says that a non-citizen who does not have a visa must be detained and must remain in detention until (a) they are given a visa or (b) they are removed from Australia. He was refused a visa. He could not bear it in Woomera and asked to be removed, rather than wait out a year or two by appealing. But it was not possible to remove him from Australia, because he was stateless: there was nowhere to remove him to. The government's argument was that, although Mr al-Kateb had committed no offence, he could be kept in detention for the rest of his life. On 6 August 2004, the High Court, by a majority of 4 to 3, accepted that argument.

The other case, heard alongside al-Kateb and decided on the same day, was Behrooz.[2] Mr Behrooz had come from Iran, sought asylum, and found himself in the endless loop of rejection and appeal, and had spent about 14 months before escaping in November 2001. At that time, Woomera was carrying three times as many people as it was designed for. The conditions were abominable. Reports from that time show that there were three working toilets for the population of nearly 1,500 people. Women having their period had to make a written application for sanitary napkins — and if they needed more than one packet, they had to write and explain why, and very often they had to go and provide the form to a male nurse, who would then dispense what they needed. The Immigration Detention Advisory Group, the government's own appointed body, described Woomera as 'a human tragedy of unknowable proportions'.

---

1   *Al-Kateb v Godwin* (2004) 219 CLR 562. (The facts underlying al-Kateb's case were actually the facts specific to a man called al Masri. For technical reasons, it was al-Kateb's case that went to the High Court)

2   *Behrooz v Secretary of the Department of Immigration* (2004) 219 CLR 486.

Mr Behrooz found it so intolerable that he escaped, along with some others. He was charged with escaping from immigration detention. The defence went like this: The Australian Constitution embodies the separation of powers. This means that the legislative power is vested in the parliament (Chapter I); the executive power is vested in the executive government (Chapter II); and the judicial power is vested in the courts (Chapter III).

As we have seen, the notion of the separation of powers involves this, that one arm of government cannot exercise the powers given to another arm. It is one of the very few constitutional safeguards we have in Australia. Central to the judicial power is the power to punish. As a matter of constitutional theory, punishment cannot be administered directly by the parliament or by the executive; punishment can only be imposed by order of the Chapter III courts. Normally, locking people up is regarded as punishment, and therefore it is only Chapter III courts that can lock people up. So, what about immigration detention?

In *Lim's* case in 1992, the High Court had held that administrative detention may be justified in limited circumstances, principally where detention is reasonably necessary as an aid to the performance of a legitimate executive function. So if a person's asylum claim is to be processed, or if the person is to be made available for removal from Australia, then, as long as the detention is reasonably necessary for those purposes, it will be lawful even though it has not been imposed by a Chapter III court.

Well, the defence in Behrooz went like this. Assuming mandatory detention is constitutionally valid, if the conditions go beyond anything that could be seen as reasonably necessary to the executive function it is said to support, that form of detention will be constitutionally invalid because it amounts to punishment inflicted by the executive.

We issued subpoenas, directed to the department and the detention-centre management company, ACM, seeking documents that would reveal details of the conditions in detention. They resisted. They said the subpoena was invalid because the conditions in detention could never affect the constitutional validity of detention. And all the way to the High Court they maintained the argument that no matter how inhumane the conditions, detention in those conditions was nevertheless constitutionally valid.

On 6 August 2004, the High Court accepted the government's argument.

Thus on the same day the High Court held that it is constitutionally valid in Australia to hold an innocent person for life in the worst conditions imaginable.

In the same year, the High Court held that the same principles apply even if the detainee is a child.[3]

These three cases from 2004 are a clear illustration of the problem that, if parliament decides to make a law that destroys basic rights, the common law is unable to prevent such a result.

'It is anti-democratic.'

In one sense, it is true that a bill of rights gives power to judges. A bill of rights limits the power of parliament, but not by reference to subject matter. A modern bill of rights introduces, or records, a set of basic values that should be observed by parliament when making laws on matters over which it has legislative power. It sets the baseline of human-rights standards on which society has agreed. Because this is so, it is wrong to say that a bill of rights abdicates democratic power in favour of unelected judges. Judges simply apply the law passed by the parliament. That is their role. Many cases raise questions about parliament's powers. Judges are the umpires who decide whether parliament has gone beyond the bounds of its power. A bill of rights is a democratically created

---

3 *Re Woolley; Ex parte Applicants M276/2003 by their next friend GS* (2004) 225 CLR 1.

document, like other statutes. Enforcing it is not undemocratic.

'It would favour minorities.'
One of the most surprising objections to a bill of rights is that it gives disproportionate power to minority groups. At one level, the complaint is accurate. In Australia today, the people whose human rights are at risk are not members of the comfortable majority, but members of minority groups who are typically powerless, and often unpopular, and almost always politically irrelevant. While a bill of rights, in terms, protects the rights of all, its primary use is to protect the rights of the weak because the strong are already safe. The criticism is all the more surprising when you consider that many of those who advance it proclaim themselves to be devout Christians. I had thought, although I haven't checked recently, that much of Christ's teaching was concerned with the protection of the weak, the unpopular, the despised, and the oppressed. It seems a curious thing, then, that practising Christians should object to a law which achieves that result.

This complaint has a darker side. Broadly speaking, Australians have a fairly respectful attitude to human rights. If most Australians were asked what they thought of human rights, they would say that human rights matter. The question then arises: how is it that those same people watched with unconcern as David Hicks languished for years in Guantanamo Bay without charge and without trial? How is it that they watched with unconcern for years as innocent men, women, and children were locked up indefinitely in desert jails merely because they were fleeing the Taliban or Saddam Hussein? How is it that we have managed such enduring complacency to the plight of the aborigines, whose land was taken and whose children were stolen? How is it that we are so indifferent to the draconian effects of the anti-terror laws as they are applied to Muslims in the Australian community, when we would not tolerate similar intrusions on our own rights?

The answer, I think, is this: Australians subconsciously divide human beings into two categories: Us and Others. We think, perhaps subconsciously, *My rights matter, and so do those of my family and friends and neighbours, but the human rights of others do not matter in quite the same way because the Others are not human in quite the same way we are*. It is dangerous thinking and profoundly wrong.

We have human rights not because we are nice or because we are white or because we are Christian, but because we are human. That's the sticking point which makes it possible for people to acknowledge that human rights matter and yet resist the possibility of those rights being protected by law.

'It would not work.'

One of the favourite back-handers used to dismiss a bill of rights is that they don't work: after all, the argument goes, the USSR had a splendid bill of rights, and so does Zimbabwe, but look what has happened in those countries. They have a point, of course, but it is not a point about a bill of rights: it is a point about the rule of law. No Constitution, no bill of rights, no statute, no other document can protect rights unless the rule of law is strong. If the political opposition is weak or absent, if the media are cowed or complacent, if the courts are not fearlessly independent, the promises contained on bits of paper will achieve nothing. That is not our problem in Australia. Our judges are competent, hard-working, and independent of the other arms of government. While I have disagreed with many judgments in Australian courts, I have never doubted the honesty or integrity of our judges. The same is not true of the USSR or Zimbabwe.

Guantanamo Bay provides both a challenge to and a demonstration of this point. President George W Bush chose Guantanamo Bay in Cuba as a place of detention specifically to avoid the reach of American courts and the principle of legality; he chose it in order to place detainees beyond the protection of the

Constitution and the Bill of Rights.

He failed. In case after case, the US Supreme Court has held that the protection of the Constitution reached Guantanamo.

Although it has taken a long time to expose the fraud and cruelty of Guantanamo, the fact that Bush chose Guantanamo, rather than some place on American soil, is mute testament to the power of a bill of rights and the rule of law. Bush chose Guantanamo in order to side-step the rule of law. The Supreme Court has gradually dismantled that plan. In the *Boumediene* case, the Supreme Court struck down that part of the Military Commissions Act which purported to deny Guantanamo detainees the right to seek habeas corpus.[4] Habeas corpus is the legal equivalent of a canary in the coal mine: when governments interfere with the right to challenge the lawfulness of a person's detention, you can be sure that all is not well.

'It would be a lawyers' feast.'

The 'lawyers' feast' argument is a popular one, because everyone hates lawyers, and everyone loves a feast. Anything that is going to make lawyers happy is a bad thing. The lawyers' feast argument is a coded way of saying that lawyers want a bill of rights because it will generate lucrative work for them. The argument is false. In Australia today, the people who need a bill of rights — the people whose rights are denied or disregarded — are almost always at the margins of society. They cannot afford to pay lawyers. Most human-rights work in Australia today is done for no fee. Some is funded so that the lawyers receive some payment — usually a very small percentage of ordinary rates. No one does human-rights work to get rich, because it cannot make you rich.

---

4 *Boumediene et al. v. Bush, President of the United States, et al.* Argued 5 December 2007 — Decided 12 June 2008.

THE FUTURE OF HUMAN RIGHTS

Human-rights arguments get short shrift in Australia. Although the Brennan enquiry, set up by Kevin Rudd when he was prime minister, recommended that Australia should have a bill of rights, Mr Rudd decided, peremptorily, that we would not have one. Australia is the only Western country not to have coherent human-rights protection, and it is the only country in the world to have turned its mind to the question in the 21st century and decided *not* to introduce it.

Meanwhile, Australia continues to abuse the human rights of asylum-seekers, of children in juvenile detention, and (it seems) of anyone suspected of being wilfully Muslim.

Perhaps the most distressing aspect of this is that, at present, a majority of Australians seem to accept that violations of basic human rights are OK. Certainly, there is general support for the policy of keeping asylum-seekers in offshore detention and preventing anyone from arriving in Australia looking for safety. Perhaps it is because they have been persuaded — by dishonest political rhetoric — that boat people are criminals from whom we need to be protected. (Fifteen years of calling boat people 'illegal', and renaming the Department 'Immigration and Border Protection' might do that.)

But perhaps there is something darker going on. Human-rights discourse really got going in the aftermath of the Second World War. Most of the major international human-rights instruments came into existence after 1945. When the concentration camps were opened, many people developed a sense that human rights mattered. But the mood shifted on 11 September 2001.

In the wake of 11 September, the USA started using Guantanamo Bay as a place where it held people, indefinitely and without trial, because they were alleged to be enemy combatants, or terrorists, or otherwise undesirable. It soon became apparent that the CIA also used torture on Guantanamo detainees. While some people protested that the use of torture was completely unacceptable, the public at large, in the USA and in Australia, appeared to think that it was worth it if it got some useful intelligence. (Generally, it does not.) When, as the Republican presidential candidate, Donald Trump announced publicly that he would reintroduce water-boarding 'and much worse', he was applauded — and upon winning office, set about reinstating it. During his first weeks as US president, Trump displayed his contempt for courts who ruled his travel-ban executive order invalid. This hints at the very troubling possibility that the rule of law in America is genuinely at risk.

It is just possible that people no longer regard human rights (apart from their own) as having much importance any more. It is just possible that human rights will be air-brushed off the map of respectable ideas, just as spiritualism (1880s–1890s) and eugenics (1890s–1930s) were once taken seriously but are no longer mentioned.

It is possible that human-rights thinking will suffer the same fate. It is possible that one day — in 10 or 20 or 50 years — people will look back and recall, without a trace of nostalgia, that there was a time when people thought about human rights; a time when Australian politicians were politically rewarded for their deliberate cruelty to refugee children.

SELF-INTEREST

The forces that produce this result, if it happens, will be the obvious, elemental forces that shape human behaviour: self-interest and fear.

One of the few, practically universal, philosophical precepts is captured in the Christian teaching 'Do unto others as you would have them do unto you.'[5] In its original Biblical expression, it says,

---

5   *New Testament* [Luke 6:31].

'[T]herefore all things whatsoever ye would that men should do to you, do ye even so to them: for this is the law and the prophets.'[6]

Described in the West as the Golden Rule, it is found in most religious and secular philosophies. It is found in Brahmanism: '[T]his is the sum of Dharma [duty]: Do nothing to others which would cause you pain if done to you.'[7] In Buddhism: '... a state that is not pleasing or delightful to me, how could I inflict that upon another?' In Confucianism: '[D]o not do to others what you do not want them to do to you.'[8] In Islam: '[N]one of you [truly] believes until he wishes for his brother what he wishes for himself.'[9] And in Taoism: '[R]egard your neighbour's gain as your own gain, and your neighbour's loss as your own loss.'[10] The same principle has been advocated by secular philosophers, including Epictetus, Plato, Socrates, Seneca, and Kant.

The foundation of the idea is reciprocity, and, in this setting, reciprocity is an expression of enlightened self-interest. Little wonder, then, that the idea is widespread. At its least, it tempers our basest impulses; at its highest, it produces acts of extraordinary altruism.

The principle of reciprocity, and the Golden Rule that springs from it, emerges from selfishness, which is a near-universal human characteristic. Human infants are near-perfect parasites: their every instinct is directed at self-preservation. It is a necessary characteristic in creatures that remain dependent on others for a very long time, unlike the infants of other species.

So, self-interest has been naturally selected because it helps us survive to adulthood. But as we grow up, we learn that the way we behave now may have consequences later. As we grow up, we

---

6   *New Testament* [Matthew 7:12].
7   *Mahabharata* [5:1517].
8   *Samyutta Nikaya* [v 353].
9   *Analects* [15:23].
10   *Imam* [13].

begin to notice that sacrificing an immediate gain in the interests of others can result in greater gains for ourselves later. We learn that it can be strategically wise to postpone or subordinate our immediate interests in favour of others.

In 1972, a book called *The Limits to Growth* was published. The book had been commissioned by The Club of Rome, and was written by Donella H. Meadows, Dennis L. Meadows, Jørgen Randers, and William W. Behrens III. It postulated that the world's population was growing exponentially, whereas the world's resources were only growing in a linear manner, which meant that at some point in the foreseeable future the world would not be able to sustain its human population.

The predictions in *The Limits to Growth* have been reviewed each five years since 1972. So far, it seems that the broad predictions of the book are borne out by experience. The human population of the world continues to grow, and it is already greater than was thought sustainable a few decades ago. At the time of writing these words (February 2017)] the world population was 7.5 billion people, and increasing by about 150,000 people *per day*. When *The Limits to Growth* was published, the world's population was 3.8 billion. (In case these numbers provoke despair, the growth rate is falling, slowly. In the 1960s, the growth rate was about 2 per cent per year. In 2017, the growth rate was about 1.1 per cent per year, and falling.)

The point of all this is simple: as we have seen, enlightened self-interest rests on an assumption of reciprocity. Reciprocity presumes that you will be or might be in the other person's position at some time in the future, so you treat the other as you might hope to be treated. As the world heads towards the limits of its carrying capacity, and as doctrinal and political conflicts erupt in various parts of the world, there is a strong inclination to pull up the drawbridge, on the assumption that we will never be forced to run for safety, and in any event we don't want to see our portion of the world's riches re-distributed from us (who have more than our share) to them (who have less).

Add fear to this — in particular, a growing fear of terrorism — and the enlightened part of self-interest starts to look different: it tends to unalloyed selfishness.

This phenomenon can be seen plainly in the way Donald Trump was received when he promised to reintroduce water-boarding 'and much worse'. Most civilised people regard torture as impossible to accept in a civilised society. But when we live in fear of being overrun by potential terrorists, the unthinkable starts to look more interesting.

But that is the tabloid view of the world and, as political parties in Australia, Britain, and the USA drift to the right, it begins to look like an uncomfortably mainstream idea. In recent years, I have been startled to be told that I am a 'rusted-on leftie' because of my work in human rights. And yet a genuine concern for human rights was in the political centre until about 20 years ago.

But in the new, post-9/11 world, it is not difficult to imagine the idea of human rights starting to look like an idea that has been overtaken by history.

Hate Mail #1

Burnside .... Christ you're a dumb fuck, dumber than dogshit, how the fuck did you ever attain a law degree?, you either printed the certificate yourself or subscribed to one of those correspondence courses from Somalia land or some equivalent dump.

Burnside .... your performance .... warrants you being certified a fucking lunatic, your diaTRIPE concerning ILLEGAL asylum seekers yet again with your condescending manner has you vilified by the majority of all Australians.

Its bullshit mate, these gate crashers need to be stopped. Let the poor people who have been lined up in refugee camps for years in here first. At least they want to work & they appreciate us & our country.

As for Tasmania, don't be so bloody stupid. How about the Tasmanians? They don't want all the rubbish dumped there.

How about you put a couple of young Afghani single gate crashers in your house for a month, see how your attitude changes then.

You are a dead set FUCKWIT

Don,t you just love do gooders and bleeding hearts with their own agendas. Send all the illegals back to their own countries .... and save all the hassle.

19

Refugees

The *Universal Declaration of Human Rights* (1948) recognised, in article 14, the right of all human beings to seek asylum in any territory they can reach. That right was recognised, presumably, because the world had come to recognise, with shame, the shocking fate of Jews, Gypsies, and others under the Nazi regime. For Europeans, especially, it was not difficult to understand two essential features of refugee movement: first, that people who are persecuted will try to escape it; and, second, that human movement from a place of oppression will generally impose a disproportionate burden on adjacent countries.

The Australian perspective was, necessarily, different. Australia is surrounded by an enormous moat. No refugees can come here on foot, and the boat ride is difficult and dangerous. But Australia had contributed very substantially to the creation of the UDHR — disproportionately for its modest population and relative unimportance back then — and it took its humanitarian obligations seriously.

In 1951, the Refugees Convention entered into force. It focussed on European refugees. In 1967, a protocol was adopted that extended the reach of the convention to refugees anywhere. The convention defines a refugee as a person who:

[O]wing to well-founded fear of being persecuted for reasons of race, religion, nationality, membership of a particular social group or political opinion, is outside the country of his nationality and is unable, or owing to such fear, is unwilling to avail himself of the protection of that country …

(It is worth noting that, while we refer un-self-consciously to 'climate refugees', that expression is not accurate. A person who is unable to return to their country because it has disappeared beneath a rising ocean is not a 'refugee' within the definition. Perhaps she should be.)

The central obligation of nations that have signed the Refugees Convention is to avoid *refoulement* — that is, returning a refugee (directly or indirectly) to a place where she may be persecuted. When the UDHR was adopted in 1948, and when the Refugees Convention was adopted in 1951, the concentration camps and the other horrors of Nazism were matters of recent memory.

THE TAMPA EPISODE

Australia's treatment of refugees took a serious turn for the worse in 2001. On 26 August 2001, the Norwegian cargo ship MV Tampa rescued the passengers of a small boat called the Palapa, which was breaking up in moderate seas in the Indian Ocean. The captain of the Tampa reckoned there might be 50 or 60 people on the Palapa. As it happened, there were 438 of them, most of whom were Hazaras from Afghanistan. The Tampa was denied entry into Australian waters; but, in defiance of prime minister John Howard, Tampa sailed into the waters off Christmas Island and into Australia's legal and political history. Howard sent out the SAS, who took command of the Tampa at gunpoint. Then there was a stand-off.

Several groups of lawyers brought proceedings in the Federal Court in Melbourne, challenging the legality of holding the people rescued by Tampa hostage on the deck of the Tampa.

The Tampa episode coincided with the terror attack on America on 11 September 2001. The judgment of Justice North in the Tampa case was handed down at 2.15 pm (Melbourne time) on 11 September 2001. The attack on America happened about eight hours later.

From that moment, there were no longer terrorists, just Muslim terrorists, and in Australia there were no longer boat people, just Muslim boat people. That attack made it plausible (although wrong) to refer to boat people as 'illegal', a strategy that persists to this day. Politically, this had three desirable qualities: it was cheap, effective, and dishonest.

To members of the public, who have no reason to look behind the things said by politicians, locking up 'illegals' as an exercise in 'border protection' makes sense. And if we treat boat people a bit harshly ... well, you can't make omelettes without breaking eggs. Once you recognise that boat people have not committed any offence by coming here, and that there is no queue, and that people fleeing terrorism are probably not terrorists themselves, it all looks different. The moral equation changes when you discover that we are mistreating frightened, innocent people.

When Tony Abbott was prime minister, and Scott Morrison was immigration minister, the rhetoric of 'illegals' became increasingly strident, and Morrison started talking about 'border protection'. The Department of Immigration and Citizenship was re-named, in Orwellian fashion, the Department of Immigration and Border Protection.

During the Tampa litigation, the Howard government established the Pacific Solution. (The unhappy resonance with the 'Final Solution' might be explained by the fact that the Pacific Solution was put together very fast, in a toxic political environment.) The Pacific Solution was put together before September 11 changed our view of the world. Mr Howard made it clear that the mandatory-detention system, and the iniquitous Pacific Solution, were designed to 'send a message'. What does this mean? It means that we treat innocent people harshly to deter others. The punishment of innocent people to shape the behaviour of others is impossible to justify. It is the philosophy of hostage-takers. Any society that is prepared to brutalise the innocent in order to achieve other objectives has stepped into a moral shadow-land.

SENDING PEOPLE BACK TO OFFSHORE DETENTION

On 3 February 2016, the High Court of Australia delivered judgment in a constitutional case (*Plaintiff M68 v Minister for Immigration and Border Protection*) that challenged the Commonwealth's legal ability to fund offshore detention. On that decision rested the fate of 267 asylum-seekers who were in Australia but faced being sent to Nauru if the challenge failed. Among the 267 people were two groups: those who had been brought from Nauru to Australia for medical treatment, and infants who had been born in Australia to women who had previously been on Nauru. By law, a baby born in Australia to an asylum-seeker mother is not entitled to Australian citizenship.

Conditions in which asylum-seekers are held on Nauru have been trenchantly criticised by various Australian and international bodies. In its 2016 report, Human Rights Watch said this of Australia's treatment of asylum-seekers:

> Australia outsources some of its obligations to asylum seekers and refugees to poorer, less well-equipped, and unsafe countries such as Nauru and Papua New Guinea (PNG). ...
>
> An AHRC report into conditions in Australian mainland immigration detention centers and facilities on Christmas Island in February found that mandatory and prolonged detention had profoundly negative impacts on the mental and emotional health

and development of children. More than 300 children committed or threatened self-harm in a 15-month period in Australian immigration detention, and 30 reported sexual assault.

Following the report's release, senior government officials made personal and unsubstantiated attacks on the credibility and integrity of the president of the AHRC, Professor Gillian Triggs, including calling for her resignation. The chairman of the International Coordinating Committee, the UN body responsible for accrediting national human rights institutions, described these attacks as intimidating and undermining the independence of the AHRC.

In March, the UN special rapporteur on torture, Juan Mendez, concluded that by failing to provide adequate detention conditions, end the practice of detaining children, and put a stop to escalating violence in processing centers, Australia was in violation of the Convention against Torture. Former Prime Minister Tony Abbott responded by stating that Australia was 'sick of being lectured by the UN'.

In 2015, Australia announced its candidacy for a seat at the UN Human Rights Council in Geneva for the 2018-2020 term. To date, with observer status at the council, Australia has a mixed record, advancing certain thematic issues but not playing a leadership role on grave country situations globally. Australia has often responded dismissively to recommendations made by UN experts about its own domestic human rights record.

In November, Australia's domestic rights record was reviewed for the second time as part of the council's Universal Periodic Review process. More than 100 countries spoke up at the review, and nearly half of them — from every corner of the globe — criticized Australia's asylum laws and refugee policies and its treatment of indigenous people.

Because New Zealand citizens bear the brunt of changes to Australia's immigration laws and face detention and deportation, criticism from New Zealand has increased. In November, New Zealand Minister of Internal Affairs Peter Dunne called Australia's immigration detention policies 'savage and inhumane' and stated that 'the modern concentration camp approach Australia has taken is simply wrong'.[1]

Former Save The Children workers on Nauru have said that children held in detention on Nauru face 'systematic violation'. Numerous bodies have said that the way asylum-seeker children are held on Nauru amounts to child abuse.

On 12 June 2015, the then prime minister, Tony Abbott, said:

What we are doing is saving life at sea. We are defending our national sovereignty, we are protecting our country from the evil trade of people smuggling, and by hook or by crook we will do what is necessary to keep our country safe and to keep this evil trade stopped.

The 2017 Global Report of Human Rights Watch was not much kinder to us:

On Nauru, refugees and asylum seekers regularly endure violence, threats, and harassment from Nauruans, with little protection from local authorities. They face unnecessary delays in, and at times denial of, medical care, even for life-threatening conditions. Many have dire mental health problems and suffer from depression. Self-harm and suicide attempts are frequent. In May 2016, two refugees self-immolated in separate incidents; one died and the other was badly burned.

At time of writing, only 25 of the 675 refugees on Manus had been allowed to move to mainland PNG, working in Lae or Port

Moresby. Of this number, several returned to Manus citing threats to personal safety and poor working and living conditions. Of six refugees who resettled from Nauru to Cambodia under an A$55 million (US$43 million) deal struck between the countries in 2015, two remain. The others returned to their country of origin.

The Australian government's offshore operations are highly secretive. Service providers working for the Australian government face criminal charges and civil penalties if they disclose information about conditions for asylum seekers and refugees. In August and September 2016, the Guardian newspaper published more than 2,000 leaked documents that exposed endemic and systematic abuse, predominantly of children, at the Nauru detention center.

In 2016, the Australian navy turned back boats carrying migrants, sending them to Vietnamese and Sri Lankan waters. Both countries have poor records concerning returned migrants.

Asylum seekers or refugees perceived to be lesbian, gay, bisexual, transgender, or intersex (LGBTI) face harassment and abuse despite the recent decriminalization of same-sex conduct in Nauru; in Papua New Guinea, such conduct remains criminalized.

In November, the Turnbull Government introduced legislation that would prohibit adult asylum seekers and refugees who have attempted to arrive in Australia by boat since July 19, 2013, from ever obtaining an Australian visa of any kind. In November, the government also announced a one-off arrangement to resettle some refugees from Manus and Nauru in the United States, saying that women, children, and families would be prioritized. At time of writing, no one had been removed for resettlement to the US.

On 3 February 2016, *Plaintiff M68* was decided in the government's favour. So here was the great moral challenge: should women, children, and Australian-born infants be sent to Nauru where, on all the evidence, the conditions constitute child abuse?

Prime Minister Malcolm Turnbull responded with fine rhetoric. In a doorstop interview on 8 February, he said:

> All of us are anxious, are anguished at the plight of children in detention. … The one thing we know we must do is manage our border protection policies, yes, with compassion, yes, with humanity, yes with a deep concern about children.
>
> But, if we make changes that have the consequence of giving the people smugglers a marketing opportunity — which they will take — they are very dangerous and agile criminals, and they use modern social media with an efficiency that is remarkable.
>
> We have to be very careful, anything we do which gives them a marketing opportunity, they will use, and they will use it to get more vulnerable people on boats and more children and their parents will die by drowning at sea.
>
> So, we have stopped the boats, and we are managing the caseload that we inherited from the Labor Party, but we have to do so — yes, with compassion, yes, yes with a passionate concern for those children. We are giving their parents every incentive to return to their country of origin, to go to settle in another country, because we know that if we give those people smugglers any marketing opportunity, let me tell you, they will use it. They will use it, and there will be more deaths at sea and more children put at risk …[2]

Now, it is easy to be distracted by the silvered delivery and the polished rhetoric. And the political reality is that Turnbull has inherited the grim logic of 15 years of demonising boat people as 'illegal'. And the Liberal party room has been fairly hostile to him.

But the worrying thing that underlies his seductive pretence at

---

2   http://malcolmturnbull.com.au/media/joint-doorstop-interview-mother-teresa-early-learning-centre

compassion is that he is prepared to send children to face abuse if that will reduce the possibility of people trying to escape persecution and reach safety in Australia. Of course, Turnbull's position (which is currently shared by the Labor Party) amounts to this: *We are so worried about you drowning, we will punish you if you don't drown. That will persuade others to stay at home and face persecution.* In short, Australia is now being candid about something that was always implicit in its mandatory-detention and offshore-processing policies: the idea of coming to Australia must be made to look worse than the prospect of facing the Taliban or ISIL.

In addition, Turnbull apparently wants people to return to the persecution they have escaped. ('We are giving their parents every incentive to return to their country of origin'.) And he said we were giving people an incentive 'to go to settle in another country'. In 2013, New Zealand had offered to resettle 300 refugees as part of a two-year deal with Australia. But in January 2016, New Zealand's immigration minister said Australia has not taken up the offer, and the resettlement places had instead been given to Syrian refugees.

Former prime minister Tony Abbott had scrapped the plan, saying the message to people smugglers had to be 'crystal clear'.

Turnbull, Abbott, and Labor leader Bill Shorten all use the same logic: treat boat people harshly, to save them from unscrupulous people-smugglers and the perils of the sea.

There are two possibilities: either they are sincere in what they say, or they are lying.

If they are sincere, they betray an unhappy lack of logic and morality. Boat people do not commit any offence by arriving, without an invitation, to seek asylum. Calling them 'illegal' is simply false. They risk their lives at sea in order to escape something worse: over the past 15 years, about 90 per cent of boat people have proved to be genuine refugees. After all, you don't risk your life at sea as a casual lifestyle choice.

And if people are desperate to avoid persecution at home, and are aware that they would face years of persecution at Australia's hands if they try to come here, experience tells us that they will try to escape to some other place.

There is nothing surprising in the idea that people who genuinely fear persecution will run for their lives. It's what people do, if they can. Whether they head to Australia, or to Europe, or somewhere else, matters much less to them than getting away from the fear of persecution.

The whole world was horrified by images of the corpse of three-year-old Aylan Kurdi after his family had fled across the Mediterranean. But those images demonstrated something we already knew: refugees perish in their attempt to find safety. If they die at the hands of their persecutors, or in the Mediterranean, or in a boat on the way to Australia, makes no difference to them: they are still dead. The main difference is in us: our national conscience (such as it is) is not troubled by seeing the broken boats, the broken corpses.

And in order to ease our conscience, we deliberately treat survivors cruelly, as a warning to those who might look to us for kindness.

But on top of this complete lack of logic, there is a profound moral failing. Australia's policy on boat people, as articulated by Turnbull on 8 February 2016, shows that we are willing to use individual, frightened human beings as instruments to help us achieve policy objectives. We are willing to sacrifice a few foreigners in order to produce a political outcome. That approach exists at the frontier where utilitarian thinking meets totalitarianism.

Minds can differ about utilitarian logic. What it means, in short, is that you do whatever produces the greatest good for the greatest number. Unfortunately, the result usually depends on the interests of the person who does the arithmetic.

The difficulty is captured in a short story by Ursula Le Guin, called 'The Ones Who Walk Away From Omelas'. It concerns an imaginary city called Omelas. In every way, Omelas is an apparently perfect society: it has beautiful architecture and music and poetry, and all of its citizens live in harmony and happiness. But when children reach adolescence, they are allowed to learn the secret that supports the beauty and happiness of Omelas. In a dungeon under Omelas there is a child, held in darkness and misery, and on the misery of that child the happiness of Omelas rests. The young teenagers are taken to see the child, so they understand fully the misery of its plight. The story ends like this:

> Often the young people go home in tears, or in a tearless rage, when they have seen the child and faced this terrible paradox. ... Their tears at the bitter injustice dry when they begin to perceive the terrible justice of reality, and to accept it. Yet it is their tears and anger, the trying of their generosity and the acceptance of their helplessness, which are perhaps the true source of the splendor of their lives. ... They know that if the wretched one were not there sniveling in the dark, the other one, the flute-player, could make no joyful music ...
>
> At times one of the adolescent girls or boys who go to see the child does not go home to weep or rage, does not, in fact, go home at all. ... (They) go out into the street, and walk down the street alone. They keep walking, and walk straight out of the city of Omelas, through the beautiful gates. They keep walking across the farmlands of Omelas. ... Each alone, they go west or north, towards the mountains. They go on. They leave Omelas, they walk ahead into the darkness, and they do not come back. The place they go towards is a place even less imaginable to most of us than the city of happiness. I cannot describe it at all. It is possible that it does not exist. But they seem to know where they are going, the ones who walk away from Omelas.

THE BORDER FORCE LEGISLATION

On 20 May 2015, the Australian parliament passed the *Australian Border Force Act*. It includes secrecy provisions that have potentially very far-reaching consequences, but it is to be hoped that these provisions will be interpreted by courts in a way that minimises their impact. The Act came into force on 1 July 2015.

Section 42 of the Act makes it an offence (punishable by two years' imprisonment) for an 'entrusted person' to 'make a record of, or disclose' protected information.

'Entrusted person' is widely defined, but it includes employees of companies that operate detention centres or provide services in detention centres, onshore or offshore.

In civil society, if a doctor becomes aware of an instance of child-sex abuse, it is a criminal offence not to report it. But if the same doctor is working in an Australian detention centre, in Australia or offshore, and becomes aware of an instance of child-sex abuse, *it is a criminal offence to report it.*

At the time of writing, no one has been prosecuted for a breach of section 42. This is so despite the fact that some brave health workers have taken a bold stand and have publicly exposed facts that they learned while working as 'entrusted persons'. The boldest and arguably the bravest challenge was an open letter published by a group of health workers, which was directed to prime minister Tony Abbott and immigration minister Peter Dutton. It read:

> Today the Border Force Act was enacted. It includes provision for a 2 year jail sentence for 'entrusted persons' such as us if we speak out about the deplorable state of human rights in immigration detention without the express permission of the Minister for Immigration and Border Protection.
>
> We have and will continue to advocate for the health of our patients despite the threats of imprisonment, because standing

by and watching substandard and harmful care, child abuse and gross violations of human rights is not ethically justifiable.

If we witness child abuse in Australia we are legally obliged to report it to the child protection authorities. If we witness child abuse in detention centres, we can go to prison for telling the media.

There are currently many issues which constitute a serious risk to the health of those to whom we have a duty of care. The Department of Immigration and Border Protection is aware of these problems and has failed to act to address them.

The Australian Health Practitioner Regulation Authority (AHPRA) has stated that, where there is a conflict between the AHPRA code of conduct and the law, we should follow the law. This can only be acceptable if the law is ethical or the code is inadequate. Neither of these is true.

We encourage others to stand firm in the face of these threats and to advocate for their patients as they are duty bound.

We challenge the Department to prosecute us, so that we may discuss these issues in open court.[3]

The authors of that letter included David Isaacs and John-Paul Sangarran, who deserve great praise for their willingness to risk their careers in order to draw attention to the iniquities of Australia's treatment of asylum-seekers.

The final paragraph of the letter is an oblique reference to the defence provided in section 48 of the Border Force Act. That section makes it a defence to a breach of section 42 if an entrusted person discloses facts learned in that capacity in a bona fide attempt to reduce a serious threat to the life or health of a person. If the authors of that letter were charged, their defence would depend on giving evidence in open court of the fact that conditions in detention, and

3 *Sydney Morning Herald*, 1 July 2015 http://www.smh.com.au/federal-politics/
   political-news/detention-centre-doctors-workers-dare-government-to-
   prosecute-them-over-new-laws-20150701-gi24pr.html

systemic abuse, were causing grave damage to the health of refugees (and detention-centre workers). The prosecution would therefore provide a public platform from which the iniquities of the detention system would be exposed to the public at large. It is highly unlikely that the court hearing the matter would order the evidence to be given in secret: open justice is one of the basic assumptions on which the court system operates.

David Isaacs, to his great credit, has taken the matter further. On 29 December 2015, he wrote to Prime Minister Malcolm Turnbull:

> I enclose a paper which I recently published in the *Journal of Medical Ethics* in which I argue that prolonged indefinite immigration detention is torture. I believe this paper, which describes what I witnessed when contracted by International Health & Medical Services (IHMS) to consult on children on Nauru, may infringe the Australian Border Force Act 2015. I invite you to prosecute me under this act so we can discuss the issue in court.
>
> If you decline to prosecute me, I invite you to repeal this regressive and repressive act which is clearly intended to suppress freedom of speech.[4]

He has not been prosecuted. Presumably, the Department of Immigration is aware of the dangers of prosecuting health workers, but prefers instead to rely on the chilling effect of the legislation.

In October 2016, the federal government announced changes to the Border Force legislation: doctors would no longer be subject to section 42 of the Act. Even so, other health workers remain subject to section 42, and they may not command the same moral authority as doctors.

It seems clear enough that the Australian Border Force Act is

---

4   The text of the letter was provided to me by David Isaacs. The fact of the letter, and the challenge it contains, was reported on ABC news on 26 January 2015 http://www.abc.net.au/news/2016-01-26/doctor-challenges-pm-over-immigration-detention-centres/7113966

designed to have a chilling effect: by frightening people who work in the detention system, the government calculates that it can keep the details of the detention system secret.

Hate Mail #2

Boxhead Burnside

I see you're up to your old tricks again Burnside.....you would have to be the greatest fuckin' dropkick of all time as a member of the legal fraternity, an already loathed institution.....you're a great role model, a vile vicious mountain of garbage, unfit to be recognised as human. ...

Must be out of work again you fuckwit eh? so you wade up to your neck in the sewers of filth to create aggressive militant publicity for yourself, oh you're a bright C**T all right Burnside. You must crave the demonisation of the majority, you love to demonstrate controversy and have no shame, only a moron would welcome that type of attention.

I'm generally preoccupied with loving, but you Burnside, I loathe that you exist, the crap that emanates from your mouth relates to your shit for brains!!!

Julienne,

you fuckin' grub, you were happy to retweet the expression, thus giving it your endorsement....I've come across rotting bodies that are less offensive than you, meanwhile, go plait ya shit!!!!

Julienne,

your sense of humour and mine don't equate, maybe this photo of ya missus at the bus stop would attest to that......defence rests!!!!

[He attached a photograph of an incredibly fat, naked woman standing at a bus-stop somewhere in America.]

20

At the margins

For people at the margins of society, the law can be especially difficult. Not only do they have limited access to legal help, their plight is often not a matter of much concern to a lot of people in the mainstream.

I had a conversation with Tim Costello some years ago that significantly changed my way of seeing things.

He told me of a time when he was running the Collins St Baptist Church. A guy who had been sleeping rough for quite a while had turned up at the church, wanting a feed. Tim was talking to him. The guy told him that that conversation was the *first time in two weeks he had had eye contact with any other human being*.

I can scarcely imagine what that must be like. That man had, at least in his own mind, completely disappeared.

I have thought about that conversation often. The idea of such alienation haunts me. But there are many people living on the margins of our society who have, at least in their own minds, disappeared. These are the people who, because of mental-health problems or simple bad luck, find themselves nursing a grievance that no one wants to hear about. The more they complain, the more they are ignored; the more they are ignored, the louder they complain. The louder they complain, the more they are avoided, viewed with suspicion. And once that cycle sets in, their problems become more and more real to them, and less and less real to those around them.

These are the people who ring late-night talkback radio, and harangue the host until even the panel operators know to filter them out. They are the new outcasts.

My conversation with Tim came in useful during the first round of Australia's panic about asylum-seekers. Between 2001 and about 2006, a lot of Australians were persuaded to be anxious about boat people arriving here. After all, the Howard government had told us they were illegals; that they had thrown their children into the sea; that they had jumped a queue somewhere. And the struggle to prevent the country from being swamped by this tide of potential terrorists was paraded as 'border protection'.

Howard recognised that there were votes to be taken from One Nation if only he could make us fear the alien horde and position himself as our protector. It worked.

There is a story told in a biography of John Howard that shows clearly what was going on. Howard was about to enter the House of Representatives to deliver his speech explaining the government's response to the Tampa. Jackie Kelly (the Liberal member for Lindsay, and one of Howard's favourites) approached him in the lobby. She said that a lot of her constituents were deserting to One Nation. Howard waved his speech in front of her and said, 'Don't worry — this will fix it'. As most people thought at the time, the government's response to the Tampa was purely political. Of course, Howard had a great run of good luck in 2001. His government refused to let the Tampa put its bedraggled cargo of rescued Hazaras ashore on Christmas Island; he cobbled together the Pacific Solution while the court case about Tampa continued. For those who did not see through the political opportunism in Howard's handling of the Tampa episode, suddenly boat people were aliens to be feared.

Of course, if the true facts were understood, our response would have seemed rather odd. It did not suit the politicians to acknowledge that boat people were not illegal, that there was no queue, that they had not thrown their children overboard, and that they were trying to escape the same extremists we were so frightened of. It still does not occur to the public at large that people fleeing terrorists are probably not terrorists themselves; that people fleeing extremists are probably not extremists themselves.

For my sins, I became involved in the issue. I was regularly asked to speak, at public events and private, about asylum-seekers. It seemed to me that the key to the problem was to explain the facts. Naïvely, I thought that most Australians would recoil at the idea of wilfully mistreating men, women, and children who had done nothing wrong but try to escape to safety.

A couple of unexpected things happened. First, as noted above, I got a few death threats. It surprised me that, having done a few fairly contentious cases in my career, I should receive death threats for going to court pro bono on behalf of people who were, self-evidently, voiceless and powerless.

And whenever I was quoted in the media as saying something outrageous like, 'It is wrong to imprison innocent children and drive them to suicide', I would receive a torrent of hate mail.

The anger and intensity of the hate mail astonished me then, and it still does. It struck me as remarkable that people would write to a complete stranger in such bluntly abusive terms. And the mail I got was seriously, vigorously abusive. (For examples of this diverting occurrence, see above.)

PRO BONO HELP

Because everyone apparently knows my name, address, and occupation, I get a large number of requests for help. I make it clear that all I can do is offer pro bono advice. I have a group of talented interns who help me deal with the problems.

It has been interesting, not to say distressing, to see the sort of troubles that plague people in our community. What is distressing is that the majority of people who write to me this way do not, in fact, have a recognisable legal or human-rights problem. Typically, they are people who have had bad luck, or have made bad choices, and find themselves trapped in a spiral of disadvantage, distress, unemployment, and mental instability. At this point, anything that looks like a legal or human-rights problem prompts them to reach out for help. I imagine that medical clinics have a similar experience.

When I reply to their approach with further questions, or with advice about what to do, it usually becomes clear that they have already been to just about every imaginable place for help: Legal Aid, a Community Legal Centre, government departments, their local doctor, or their local MP. No one can help them, because they have no single, clear problem. Part of their distress is caused by feeling so isolated.

The most distressed, and distressing, group are people who are probably paranoid schizophrenics. One person who has written to me quite often is convinced that the police, and other government agencies, are spying on him all the time. He is intelligent and well-educated. He sends me video footage of ordinary street scenes, at the traffic lights, in shopping centres, in suburban streets, and he asserts (and no doubt believes) that various people captured on his videos are in fact plain-clothes operatives — stalking him, watching him, keeping him in a kind of open prison. He points out, rationally enough, that such conduct is a serious breach of his human rights. And if the innocuous scenes he sends did in fact show what he sees, he would be right. But they do not show what he sees. They prove nothing at all. He insists that the Commonwealth government has a secret control order against him: but he can offer no explanation how a control order can work, if it is kept secret from everyone.

The difficulty with people like this man is that they cannot be convinced that their view of the facts does not line up with reality. And it is hard for any lawyer to tell a would-be client that he needs psychiatric help.

The end-result is that people like him get pushed from pillar to post but rarely, if ever, do they get the help they actually need.

There are only a couple of bright spots in this dismal tale.

The first concerns a woman who turned up in my chambers one lunchtime, quite distressed and anxious to speak to me. We chatted for a bit, but the long and short of it was that she had been receiving treatment for paranoid schizophrenia, and her treatment had been interrupted; she had become convinced that her treating doctor was trying to kill her with the medication he had prescribed, so she had decided not to take it any more. She wanted me to mind the diary she had been keeping because she was confident that she would soon be killed, and she wanted me to have the evidence that would identify the guilty party.

We spoke for some time about schizophrenia. I suggested that perhaps she could go to the opposite side of town from where she lived, and see a GP, ask the GP for a referral to a psychiatrist, and promise herself that she would take whatever medication that psychiatrist suggested. After all, the prospect of that person being in league with the psychiatrist she thought was trying to kill her was almost zero. She agreed to think about it, and she left my chambers. In the meantime, I promised to look after her diary, although I was fairly sure her psychiatrist was not in fact trying to kill her, and fairly sure she would not follow my advice.

About two months later, she turned up again. She had, in fact, done as I suggested. She had been to another psychiatrist. She had taken the medication he prescribed. She was feeling a lot better, and realised that she had misjudged her original doctor. In the circumstances, she did not need me to look after her diary any more.

How odd that one of my few successes in the field of human rights should result from a modicum of medical knowledge and a bit of common sense.

The second bright spot is this. Most of the people who write asking for pro bono help have simply not got a legal problem. While they may have had a genuine legal problem in the past, typically it is buried in history, and the statutory time limit for bringing legal action expired years or decades before. The real problem is that their lives have gone off track, and they no longer feel any connection to the society that has let them down so badly. A surprising number of these people seem to benefit from having their problem taken seriously, from getting written advice in response to their letter, or from being listened to for half an hour.

It is a powerful reminder of what great work the Community Legal Centres do. Underfunded and under-resourced, they exist in order to help people deal with legal problems, but in many cases the real help they give lies in the fact that they extend the simple dignity of listening to a person's distress. They help rescue the alienated. I am hugely impressed with Community Legal Centres. They deserve to be better funded and better recognised for the work they do.

Of course, there are plenty of people in the community who have genuine legal problems who cannot afford legal representation: people who face minor criminal charges, but cannot afford a lawyer; people who have a good civil claim to make, or a good defence to a civil claim brought against them, and cannot afford legal representation.

ACCESS TO JUSTICE

Access to justice is a cornerstone of any democracy. Access to justice must include the right to participate meaningfully in the legal system.

The legal system in Australia is an adversary system: competing parties advance evidence and arguments, and the court sits as an impartial umpire to decide the dispute. The adversary system assumes that both parties are competently represented: that is its most basic assumption. If that assumption fails, the system fails. Our system struggles to work properly when one party is unrepresented. But litigation is expensive, and many people can't afford it.

Legal Aid is the government's way of making good the political promise of access to justice, but Legal Aid is already underfunded, and cuts to Legal Aid guarantee that for many people access to justice is nothing but a political slogan.

The government is spending increasing amounts on police and Public Safety Officers. Their increased numbers result in more citizens being brought before courts. Those people need legal representation, but the government refuses to fund Legal Aid properly.

Thousands of self-represented litigants come before courts every year. This imposes unreasonable strains on judges, and it makes cases longer and more difficult than they should be. It often leads to mistakes. Twenty-five per cent of all appeals involve unrepresented litigants. It wastes vast amounts of judicial and other resources.

People who face a court unrepresented suffer an immediate disadvantage. Only by good luck will they get the result they might have got if they had been represented. And even assuming the court reaches the right decision, it is likely that the unrepresented litigant will have understood almost nothing of the process, and will leave with a rankling sense of injustice. With some justification, those people will leave court feeling that the system is not working, at least not for them. They become aliens in their own land.

But they are not alone.

Since 2001, Australian politicians have won electoral popularity by taking a tough line on asylum-seekers. Refugees who try to navigate the legal system alone, in order to get a just result, face a truly daunting task. But lawyers who act for asylum-seekers are sometimes the target of abuse. The abuse often comes from people who feel that their quest for justice is more important, or more deserving, than that of refugees. This overlooks the fact that justice is equally important to everyone. Politicians may not be inclined to help refugees in their quest for justice, perhaps because they fear a political backlash. But they should notice how many Australians — people who vote — are shut out from justice because Legal Aid and Community Legal Centres are so grossly under-funded.

During the past 15 years, asylum-seekers have been hoisted to a position of public hatred that has made it politically possible for governments to treat them with increasing harshness, and made it politically necessary for Labor, in opposition, to support these measures. Without any protest from the press or the public, the Howard government succeeded in establishing, in the courts, that the central elements of its deterrent policy were legally valid.

Not enough people know the cases of Ahmed al-Kateb and Mehran Behrooz. (I discuss them on pages 185–7.) Together, they show how harshly Australian laws treat refugees who come to Australia without an invitation, and how limited are the powers of the courts to ameliorate that harshness.

The Rudd government in 2008 introduced significant changes in the treatment of asylum-seekers. They were welcomed by those of us who felt that the values of the nation had been betrayed by the Howard government. In retrospect, it may be that Rudd could afford to be nice to asylum-seekers because none were arriving. Things changed in 2009, after Mr Abbott had won leadership of the Coalition and started talking tough about asylum-seekers.

The 2013 election saw both major political parties engaged in a competition to outdo each other in their promises to mistreat boat people. The theory was that this would deter others from seeking protection in Australia.

Promising to treat innocent people badly is not usually a vote-winner. In most cases, it would be seen as a mark of depravity.

But the argument starts at the wrong place. It starts with the Coalition's oft-repeated statement that boat people are 'illegals'. It starts from the language of 'border protection' and 'queue-jumping': language calculated to make the public think that boat people are undesirables, people to be feared, people we need to be protected from.

The fact is that boat people do not break any law by coming here the way they do. Over the past 15 years, more than 90 per cent of them have ultimately been assessed (by us) as refugees entitled to our protection. An estimated 25,000 boat people arrived in Australia in the 12 months to 30 June 2013. That represents only four weeks' ordinary population growth. For comparison, in the year ended December 2012 over six million visitors came to our shores (mostly for tourism or business), and we received 168,685 new permanent migrants. Boat people do not present a demographic problem for us.

Spooked by tabloid scare-mongering, both major parties have chosen deterrent policies: call them 'illegal', treat them harshly, push them off to our small, impoverished Pacific neighbours.

The spectacular cost of these measures passes without complaint because it is seen as a kind of protection. While it is difficult to separate out the various components of the cost, indefinite detention in Nauru or Manus costs about A$500,000 per person per year. The actual cost varies: metropolitan detention is cheapest. It gets more and more expensive as the place of detention is more remote, and offshore detention is the most expensive, but that is the currently preferred model. On current estimates, we spend between $2 billion and $5 billion each year brutalising people who have committed no offence and have done nothing worse that ask for protection. While $5 billion is a vast, nearly unimaginable, number for most people, there is another unit of measure. Our detention system costs about one million Geelong chopper rides a year![1]

---

1   In 2015, Bronwyn Bishop visited Geelong, which is one hour's drive south of Melbourne. She left her Commonwealth driver and instead took a helicopter there and back, at a cost to taxpayers of about $5,000. She maintained that she had done nothing wrong. As an example of fiscal restraint, it was a failure.

THE AUSTRALIAN MYTH

Australia has constructed a myth about itself that cannot survive unless we forget a number of painful truths. We draw a veil of comforting amnesia over anything that contradicts our self-image.

We forget that boat people who come here to ask for protection are not illegal in any sense — they are exercising the right that every person has in international law to seek asylum in any country they can reach.

We forget that the greatest number of unauthorised boats to arrive in a single day got here in January 1788.

We forget that many of the first white settlers in this country were true illegals: sent here by English courts for a range of criminal offences, together with the soldiers sent to guard them, and the administrators who, following London's instructions, stole the country from its original inhabitants who (if possession is nine points of the law) had the backing of 40,000 years of law to justify calling the white invaders 'illegals'.

And we forget, too, the line in the second verse of our national anthem. For those who come across the sea, there truly are boundless plains to share. For refugees locked away in remote detention centres, that line must cast light on the frontier where delusion meets hypocrisy.

PEOPLE-SMUGGLERS

When today's refugees wash up on our shores, politicians speak with concern about the boat people who die in their attempt to get to safety. But their concern is utterly false. Instead of attacking the refugees directly, which is their real purpose, they attack the people-smugglers instead. Because, aren't people-smugglers the worst people imaginable, the 'scum of the earth'? They forget that Oskar

Schindler was a people-smuggler. So was Dietrich Bonhoeffer. And so was Gustav Schroeder, captain of the ill-fated *MS St Louis*, which left Hamburg in May 1939 with a cargo of 900 Jews looking for help. Schroeder tried every trick in the book to land his passengers somewhere safe, but was pushed away. He ended up putting them ashore again in Europe, and more than half of them perished in concentration camps. Captain Schroeder was a people-smuggler, but was also a hero, and if the world had not been so harsh he would have been a saviour.

And we forget that, without the help of people-smugglers, refugees are left to face persecution or death at the hands of whatever tyranny threatens them. Let Turnbull or Shorten say publicly that, in the same circumstances, they would not use a people-smuggler if they had to.

Many recent boat people are Hazaras from Afghanistan. They are targeted ruthlessly by the Taliban, who are bent on ethnic cleansing. The Hazara population of Afghanistan has fallen dramatically over the past decade, as Hazaras escape or are killed. The Taliban want to get rid of all of them. We have forgotten that we are locked in mortal combat with the Taliban.

So here we are. We have forgotten our origins and our good fortune; we are blind to our own selfishness. In place of memory, we cling to a national myth of a generous, welcoming country, a land of new arrivals where everyone gets a fair go — a myth in which vanity fills the emptiness where the truth was forgotten.

During the 2013 election campaign, many of us watched aghast as both major parties promised mistreatment so harsh that it would act as a deterrent; mistreatment so unpleasant that it would seem more attractive to stay home and face down the Taliban rather than flee for safety. It was, and remains, the only election in Australian history in which promises of cruelty to human beings were used to attract votes. It is not difficult to imagine that promising cruelty to animals might not have worked the same way.

It is painful to recognise that we are now a country which would brutalise one group with the intention that other people in distress will prefer not to ask us for help.

The sight of the major parties competing to promise greater cruelty to boat people is new in Australian politics. We have never been perfect, but this was something without precedent.

But some of us remember how things once were. Some of us see how things could be.

21

What is to be done?

Acts of injustice done,
Between the setting and the rising sun
In history lie like bones, each one
—WH Auden, *The Ascent of F6*

T he gap between the legal system and the justice system is too wide. Whatever theory of justice you might have, the fact is that injustice is more common in our society than we would like to admit.

What can be done?

The legal system works well: Australian lawyers are competent and hard-working; Australian judges are honest and diligent. Legal education is well designed and thorough. Most lawyers are concerned about injustices in the system; many more lawyers do pro bono work than the public realise. Despite its bleak reputation, the legal profession is, by and large, competent and well motivated.

But most of the instances of injustice discussed in this book are not caused by lawyers: they are caused by parliaments. As noted earlier, in our system of government, parliaments are the supreme law-makers. If they make bad laws, the result will be seen by some (sometimes by most) as unjust. For this, there are only two possible solutions.

The first is to have well-designed protection for fundamental rights and values. A modern bill of rights goes a long way towards this. If we had this, lawyers would have something effective to work with when trying to help a client who faces serious injustice. But the history of rights protection in Australia suggests that comprehensive protection of basic human rights in Australia will be difficult to achieve, and may not be achieved (or even approached) for a long time.

The second is to fix our political system. Partisan politics in Australia is not working properly. The rise of the right across Western civilisation (seen, for example, in the Brexit vote, the election of Donald Trump as president of the United States, the resurgence of Pauline Hanson, and even the possibility that Marine Le Pen might have become president of France) suggests that the lessons of 1933–1945 have been forgotten. Syrian refugees are increasingly unwelcome in Europe, despite harrowing footage of the destruction of Mosul and Aleppo.

In Australia, it is hard to avoid the conclusion that most (not all) of our federal parliamentarians are motivated more by a desire to gain and hold power than by a desire to pursue and implement policies to which they have a genuine philosophical attachment. The fact that both the Liberal–National Coalition and the Labor Party have adopted nearly identical positions on boat people suggests that a majority in each party machine is more concerned with winning than with decency, justice, or any other high ideal.

Curiously, when challenged about current contentious matters (such as the role of Centrelink, the funding of Community Legal Centres, refugee policy, and skilled-worker visa policies), the Coalition's standard response is to blame the former Labor government. This overlooks a couple of important things. First, Labor and Coalition policies are strikingly similar. Second, Labor lost government in 2013, so the Coalition has had years to fix things if it was inclined to.

If we care about justice, we need to remember that it is individual people who suffer injustice. Securing justice is, from first to last, a concern for the treatment of the individual. But it seems that politicians are not, these days, much interested in the individual: they are interested in the party machine, and the party machine is interested in the majority, since they can only hope to win or hold government at the pleasure of the majority. If the majority do not care about injustices suffered by Aborigines or Muslims, or the disabled or the unemployed, governments will tolerate continued injustices suffered by those groups.

If we care about justice, we need to fix our political system. In the past, the acid test of a political policy was 'Is it right?' These days, the test is 'Will it sell?' That becomes: 'Will it attract the support of the tabloid press?' But that does not produce democracy: it produces mob rule. And where the mob rules, individuals will suffer, and justice will perish.

Injustices that are avoidable but tolerated are like canaries in the mine: they are a warning of worse things to come.

For those of us who do not live at the margins, it is useful to recall the famous observation of Martin Niemöller during a lecture after World War II:

First they came for the Socialists, and I did not speak out —
Because I was not a Socialist.

Then they came for the Trade Unionists, and I did not speak out —
Because I was not a Trade Unionist.

Then they came for the Jews, and I did not speak out —
Because I was not a Jew.

Then they came for me — and there was no one left to speak for me.

Appendices

Crying out for help

Life at the margins is not easy. Most Australians will never experience it. Most Australians do pretty well. Most Australians will never experience a denial of their basic human rights.

But for those who have been driven to the margins by poverty or ill-health or mental illness, life looks very different. All of us owe it to them to have some regard for what the world looks like from their position. Justice is only rarely available to people on the margins. When it is available, it is generally because of the work of unsung heroes who work in community legal centres or the Legal Aid office.

In the next few pages, I set out just a few examples of the many requests for help I receive by mail. It is impossible to read them and not feel a sense of concern that people with problems like these are not better cared for in our lucky country.

It is obvious that many of them do not have a legal problem — at least, not a problem that the law can solve, because the facts are so ancient, or so elusive, or so unlikely ever to be proved.

But the person writing undoubtedly has a problem. It is tempting to think that a number of them have a psychiatric problem, but that's not my speciality, so I can't make that assessment. But whatever the nature of the problem, it is still a problem, and one that deserves attention and concern.

Dear Sir,

Can you help me?

I was born into a family with corrupt connections to the police and intelligence communities. One of these has just been convicted of murder.

As I turned out to be cut from different cloth, and because i have (unsolicited) knowledge of their criminality (since 1975), I have been subject to long term surveillance and harassment because of my refusal to take a bribe or be a 'team player'.

I'm currently subject to long term gang stalking, some of which i suspect is tax payer funded.

I have taken some recent counter-surveillance photos, see attached. I also have photos going back to 2002.

I've made complaints to the police over the years who do nothing.

* * *

Dear Mr Burnside

I sent then Prime Minister Mr Abbott proof that 7.8 million dollars of taxpayers money was given to two developers, he replied within a few days telling me to give the information to Mr Christopher Pyne. I did sent full details to Mr Pyne, after several months and many email asking him to respond he eventually replied, telling me to go and speak to the highbrow thieves who gave taxpayers money to two of their developer mates. Yes me speak to them, I kid you not.

I read that Mr Brandis told Senator Bill Heffernan that 'no Australian was above the law', so I sent full details of the crime to Mr Brandis, no reply. Full details were sent to our new Prime Minister Mr Turnbull, no reply. I then reported the crime to fraud@pmc.gov.au Ms Candice Milosevic was of course interested and asked me to send her full details which I did, all of a sudden the investigation stopped. Now, I wonder who had enough clout to pull the plug. The arrogance of these overpaid dishonest lot is mind boggling, how dare they not respond to this disgraceful crime.

The arrogance of these highbrow thieves tells me that they have been getting away with this for years and will continue to get away with it because they have the highest level of power in this country covering up for them. They didn't even attempt to hide the crime just the blatant 'misappropriation of funds' a staggering amount of nearly 8 million dollars. Naïve little me thought if the Liberals aren't interested, Mr Shorten will run with it, I sent him all the details, no reply. …

You will love this, I sent the details to an Integrity Commissioner after several emails asking him to respond I received this reply … he could only investigate 'misconduct' — which has a specific definition. Really Commissioner, I thought stealing had a very specific definition.

* * *

I wish to bring to your attention matters involving serious, premeditated and systemic abuse of human rights by official entities in all Australian states and territories. Note that the issues are not confined to Australia, in fact identical issues exist in the USA and Canada (see National Association to Stop Guardianship Abuse)

I would greatly appreciate any advice and assistance you can provide. Given that the several thousands of matters of which my group is aware are probably only the tip of the iceberg, we believe the services of a competent human rights barrister would assist in restoring victims control of their lives and forcing the procedural changes that are desperately needed. Some of us plan on visiting victims in other states in the near future with a view to increasing group numbers.

The attached document provides an overview of the matter of immediate concern to me; this is only one of several thousand matters involving QCAT.

My view in light of considerable experience with QCAT matters is that the tribunal is corrupt to the core and consequently any expenditure whether time or financial expended on pursuing justice within the kangaroo court will be completely wasted. What we need urgently is to get the matter moved to the Supreme Court which must pay at least lip service to rules of evidence, and ideally moved to a court outside Queensland where (hopefully) there will be a disconnect from the corruption endemic to Queensland. The (Queensland) *Guardianship and Administration Act* 2000 provides that capacity must be assumed at every review and this capacity can only be rebutted with cogent and current evidence of incapacity. The most relevant authority is probably *Bucknall* QSC09-128 in which the Supreme Court held that an earlier finding of incapacity was irrelevant ... what was required was current evidence, and in the absence of same the tribunal had no option but to return a finding of capacity.

I have been accused several times of having a somewhat jaded view of the legal profession, in fact I brought the ceiling down in a legal ethics lecture when I suggested the terms 'legal' and 'ethics' are mutually incompatible. It is evident that lawyers and the judiciary love to twist the law into unrecognizable forms with a view to convincing victims that something that is obviously white, is actually black. In this case, I suggest that *Bucknall* constitutes a binding precedent that QCAT has no option but to recognize. One issue I believe impacts on the effectiveness of lawyers in QCAT is that any claim of malpractice on the part of a lawyer in Queensland is likely to heard within QCAT, consequently lawyers are paranoid about not offending QCAT. I've been advised by Queensland based lawyers several times that *Bucknall* won't be considered relevant by QCAT and to date no lawyer I've consulted has been prepared to argue in favour of the *Bucknall* matter ...

* * *

Dear Sir

I know you are a very Busy person and I thank you for your time, I am writing to you because I have heard you sometimes take on hardluck cases like mine or rather cases like mine where one has been the target when the abuse of authority is involved

The following is an account of an incident/assault/bashing of me by federal PSO's at Sydney airport Oct 31 2008. (a month before a bike was bashed and killed at the same airport and the PSO's took 20min to get there inspite being forewarned when the plain left melbourne an hour earlier, I only mention this to highlight how it is so easier for the PSO's to earn their KPI brownie points attacking disable people than attending a real incident like the cowards they are)

Please help restore my faith in authority and the system, I, as someone who has served in the Army, before I go to my grave, would like to believe that my service was not for nothing

the account has been rendered over time and edited so may seem a little disjointed

It has been so long as it has taken me this long to feel strong enough in spite of having cancer now to try to get what I am entitled and was denied due to the corruption of officials

Oct 2016

currently under treatment for cancer

I am writing this to you in a last hope to have some justice in that I am the subject of a gross miscarriage of justice

I hope you will do me the honour of reading this through and speaking with me before making any decision

What follows has been edited and added to (as memory permits) since the incident on Oct 31 2008

attacked at sydney airport by PSOs for asking for a walking stick, hospitalised in the mental wing when they knew they hurt me physically and that I had physical problems, threatened with the anti terror laws and put through 2 years of court so they could protect their lying asses as they clearly perjured themselves in order to pervert justice, after 2 years of hearings and obstruction by them they lost and were ordered to pay my costs of near 40,000 but appealed having to pay the costs on the grounds they believed they could win, and the judge [xxx] decided their perjury and perversion of justice was perfectly acceptable to base for a conclusion that they could win, and refused my costs, now $45,000

after feds so called interview, being interviewed by those that attacked me!!!, an interview recorder that didn't work???, the feds sent me back to the mental ward in the back of a divvy van knowing I had back problems and did the movie thing of swerving around corners deliberately to throw me from side to side, I could hear them laughing in front. When I fell out of the van on the ground and not able to get up all I got was 'go on get up you know you can' and finally when the realised I couldn't they ('THE SO CALLED PHSYKE PEOPLE') got a camode to sit me in instead of a wheelchair, deliberately degrading and the PSHYK doctor was present all the while and condoning the behaviour

after feds and fucking hospital finished with me I was basically dumped in sydney with nowhere to stay and no way to get home, ended up at central station to try to get a train home, after midnight sometime I collapsed in the terminal and was on the floor for near on 2 hours(I believe I may have been unconscious for a time) before the pain had eased enough for me to hobble somewhere else in the station to sleep on the floor, bear in mind my walking aides were destroyed and I was without them

the question that Judge [xxx] failed/refeused to address is:- is asking for your rights under law or rather, being assaulted in breach of these laws, OH&S law and Dissability discrimination law, deemed to be me causing a disruption and putting the airport at risk

I had said as they were bashing me why don't you just get it over and kill me. I was already in a lot of pain before I got to the security point, but then I was assaulted and put into even more pain when I was denied my walking aides or any substitute. this pain doesn't just simply go away when they eventually and casually returned my stick. And then I was attacked and pushed backwards over the conveyor, from this point I was essentially in shock from the pain and just wanted the pain to end, yet !!!!! while I am being bashed??????. Having this statement used as an excuse to send me to a mental hospital is just to cover their corruption and unprovoked attack on me. Apparently I am not the first to have this done, seems a matter of process by the feds so as to obviscate any contribution to events on their behalf, by having people labelled as nut cases.

RE COURT DOC FROM [xxx]

denied compensation because they believed they could win. A belief founded solely on the perjury of their officers in the first case and the fabrication created by all those involved. It took them 6 months to find something to charge me with, 6 welll 8 months by the time I got their call to say what what I was being charged for, some female officer. 8 years down the track and I can remember that I was on my motorbike heading to melboure from castlemaine and near sunbury where I pulled over, which in fact makes it closer to 8 months

[xxx] makes the ASSUMPTION that if it is not in the video that it did happen as the PSO/SMP say, in spite of proof they lied in court; the premis [xxx] is acting on is that I am guilty until proven innocent. WHERE IS THE PRESUMPTION OF INNOCENCE THAT IS FUNDEMENTAL TO AUSTRALIAN LAW HERE and that of a free and democratic society The whole case should never have been brought against me in the first incidence due to all of their incompetence and lies

No independent witnesses were ever interviewed even though there were a number of them, they would have supported my position that I was deliberately attacked and mistreated from the very beginning which is exactly why they were not interviewed . Only witnesses with vested interests/involvement were interviewed and summoned in the original court to provide evidence, ie the smp security

As for the interview, there is the recording/ they could not get the machine to work. My answers were always the same as I repeated over and over again the sequence of events that happened as I did in the court and never deviated. My statement coincided exactly with what was on the video, I have a very good eye and mind for detail most of the time given I design highly detailed scale models. Where they got the Q & As from in the court doc I have no idea, fabricated again.

My state of mind was a DiIRECT RESULT of THEIR actions(in the first instance) from the very beginning with the assault of taking my walking aides from me in breach of OH&S and Discrinination laws of this country.

The cause of the incident was totally DISREGARDED by [xxx] and that was the FAILURE of SMP & PSOs to comply with OH & S and Dissability laws, deliberately and calculated, putting MY SAFETY at risk. and their failure to comply with existing proceedures for disabled by doing a pat down search which I since found out was the proceedure they were required to do but were too god damn lazy and inconvenienced to perform

The failure of the PSOs of identifying unusual behaviour when I turned around and went back to the counter to ask for the supervisor, this is when they the PSO's should have intervened and approached me and aske if the were a problem, IN COMPLIANCE WITH THEIR PROCEEDURES. Also they failed to follow their proceedures when approaching someone they believed to have a weapon, MY WALIKING STICK THEY CLAIMED, by asking me to put the weapon on the ground. They simply attacked, I had already thrown my stick to the ground as the first thing I knew there was a problem was angry voices yelling 'this ones not flying today' as the 3 of them charged at me, me, someone who was obviously physically impaired I immediately threw my stick to the ground to comply with their proceedures that they themselves were disregarding totally

They Failed in their 'DUTY OF CARE' yet another thing [xxx] REFUSED to consider

[xxx] also REFUSED to consider testimony from a prosecution witness that would have supported my case that of ROCOCO

[xxx] DISMISSED the behaviour of SMP security and that is when the assault on me began, as IRRELEVENT, does this judge make his decisions based on the premis that it is OK to persecute and bully disabled people contrary to the law of australia, but to make all his assumptions in favour of the bullies 'SMP & PSOs' with the assumption that I am guilty and have to prove my innocence

[xxx] makes the ASSUMPTION thAT witnesses to the bashing in the video without interviewing them, were shocked at my behaviour and rather, not shocked at the behaviour of the PSO's in their treatment of a disabled person in their all out attack on me. yet none of these people were ever interviewed (because their statements would have supported my position that I was attacked without provocation or reason or due process)

were the witnesses interviewed … Of course not, as those witnesses would have supported my position, so how can a judge again come from the position of assuming GUILTY UNTILL PROVEN INNOCENT. Feds consciously chose not to interview independent witnesses, just the ones directly involved in the incident and attack on me thus ensuring a cover up, which they had vested interest in, covering up their bullying

Detail — the truth is in the detail and [xxx] IGNORES the

detail in favour of the interests of CORRUPT lying PSO's and SMP. the kind of use of facts by [xxx] goes like this. the judge [xxx] has 2 feet, a duck has 2 feet, therefore the judge [xxx] is a duck. and this is the kind of intelligent assessment that has denied me justice at the hands of [xxx] since his hearing in 2010

It seems very much like a 'WHITE' judge([xxx]) is overturning the decision of a black 'JUDGE' ([yyy]) because I am not black and there would be no outcry of racism because I am white and we can bury this cripple in costs and so protect our corrupt officials (PSO's & SMP)

People wonder why I would move to the US if I could, well I live in a country that has laws that make it legal to murder gay men. you can add to my being denied my rights by the fact that is is still legal for straight men to murder gay men and use the excuse of 'GAY PANIC' as a defence.

life pretty much from this point has been downhill with persistent night and daymares, suicide attempts and severe depression

as a result of PTSD from that bashing, I have constant day and nightmares which have resulted in at least a couple of real attempts of ending my life in order to get the violence of protecting myself out of my head

I don't know what you can do for me or if you are even willing to try as I know I have no way of paying unless you were to win for me, I AM seeking compensation for what this has done to me, it seems the only way government departments will change policy is if it costs them. I have been a disabled pensioner since 1998 and also an ex serviceman not that that is really relevant except that I have a high sense of integrity and sense of right and wrong and I believe I have been seriously wronged by a this gross miscarriage of justice; and if there were any way I could pay you to take this on for me I would

* * *

Hi Julian

My name is … I'm from Ireland but I'm living in Cambridge I was wondering if you could help me two devices where planted in my mouth a good few years ago I've lost the two devices but I've got camera evidence and I've still got a bit of the device in my gum to prove that they where in my mouth they are also using mind control and they have cameras in my eyes because they say the see everything I see and I seen the camera evidence on a nurses phone in a mental home I've been getting tortured for years and I'm on to there operations and projects like I was reading something last night on Facebook about human trafficking and hotel rooms there are a lot of people in America who are micro chipped and are wearing tracking devices so are the underground able to fly under the reader while being detected and I was talking about these methods a few years ago on Facebook why are they not using them are they working hand & hand

Try to imagine what life is like for these people. And then imagine what it is like for them to be turned away every time they seek help.

Appendix B

Codifying and protecting human rights

I. PRINCIPAL CONTENTS OF UNIVERSAL DECLARATION OF HUMAN RIGHTS

Whereas recognition of the inherent dignity and of the equal and inalienable rights of all members of the human family is the foundation of freedom, justice and peace in the world,

Whereas disregard and contempt for human rights have resulted in barbarous acts which have outraged the conscience of mankind, and the advent of a world in which human beings shall enjoy freedom of speech and belief and freedom from fear and want has been proclaimed as the highest aspiration of the common people,

Whereas it is essential, if man is not to be compelled to have recourse, as a last resort, to rebellion against tyranny and oppression, that human rights should be protected by the rule of law, ...

Article I   All human beings are born free and equal in dignity and rights. They are endowed with reason and conscience and should act towards one another in a spirit of brotherhood. ...

Article 2	Everyone is entitled to all the rights and freedoms set forth in this Declaration, without distinction of any kind, such as race, colour, sex, language, religion, political or other opinion, national or social origin, property, birth or other status. Furthermore, no distinction shall be made on the basis of the political, jurisdictional or international status of the country or territory to which a person belongs, whether it be independent, trust, non-self-governing or under any other limitation of sovereignty.
Article 3	Everyone has the right to life, liberty and security of person.
Article 4	No one shall be held in slavery or servitude; slavery and the slave trade shall be prohibited in all their forms.
Article 5	No one shall be subjected to torture or to cruel, inhuman or degrading treatment or punishment.
Article 6	Everyone has the right to recognition everywhere as a person before the law.
Article 7	All are equal before the law and are entitled without any discrimination to equal protection of the law.
Article 8	Everyone has the right to an effective remedy by the competent national tribunals for acts violating the fundamental rights granted him by the constitution or by law.
Article 9	No one shall be subjected to arbitrary arrest, detention or exile.
Article 10	Everyone is entitled in full equality to a fair and public hearing by an independent and impartial tribunal, in the determination of his rights and obligations and of any criminal charge against him.
Article 11	1. Everyone charged with a penal offence has the right to be presumed innocent until proved guilty

according to law in a public trial at which he has had all the guarantees necessary for his defence.

Article 12 No one shall be subjected to arbitrary interference with his privacy, family, home or correspondence, nor to attacks upon his honour and reputation. Everyone has the right to the protection of the law against such interference or attacks.

Article 13 1. Everyone has the right to freedom of movement and residence within the borders of each State.

Article 14 1. Everyone has the right to seek and to enjoy in other countries asylum from persecution.

Article 15 1. Everyone has the right to a nationality.

Article 16 1. Men and women of full age, without any limitation due to race, nationality or religion, have the right to marry and to found a family.

Article 17 1. Everyone has the right to own property alone as well as in association with others.

2. No one shall be arbitrarily deprived of his property.

Article 18 Everyone has the right to freedom of thought, conscience and religion; this right includes freedom to change his religion or belief, and freedom, either alone or in community with others and in public or private, to manifest his religion or belief in teaching, practise, worship and observance.

Article 19 Everyone has the right to freedom of opinion and expression; this right includes freedom to hold opinions without interference and to seek, receive and impart information and ideas through any media and regardless of frontiers.

Article 20 1. Everyone has the right to freedom of peaceful assembly and association. …

Article 21 1. Everyone has the right to take part in the government of his country, directly or through freely chosen representatives. ...

Article 22   Everyone, as a member of society, has the right to social security and is entitled to realization, through national effort and international co-operation and in accordance with the organization and resources of each State, of the economic, social and cultural rights indispensable for his dignity and the free development of his personality.

Article 23   1. Everyone has the right to work, to free choice of employment, to just and favourable conditions of work and to protection against unemployment.

2. Everyone, without any discrimination, has the right to equal pay for equal work.

Article 24   Everyone has the right to rest and leisure, including reasonable limitation of working hours and periodic holidays with pay.

Article 25   1. Everyone has the right to a standard of living adequate for the health and well-being of himself and of his family, including food, clothing, housing and medical care and necessary social services, and the right to security in the event of unemployment, sickness, disability, widowhood, old age or other lack of livelihood in circumstances beyond his control. ...

Article 26   1. Everyone has the right to education. ...

Article 27   1. Everyone has the right freely to participate in the cultural life of the community. ...

2. PRINCIPAL CONTENTS OF INTERNATIONAL COVENANT ON CIVIL AND POLITICAL RIGHTS

The States Parties to the present Covenant,

Considering that, in accordance with the principles proclaimed in the Charter of the United Nations, recognition of the inherent dignity and of the equal and inalienable rights of all members of the human family is the foundation of freedom, justice and peace in the world,

Recognizing that these rights derive from the inherent dignity of the human person,

Recognizing that, in accordance with the Universal Declaration of Human Rights, the ideal of free human beings enjoying civil and political freedom and freedom from fear and want can only be achieved if conditions are created whereby everyone may enjoy his civil and political rights, as well as his economic, social and cultural rights,

Considering the obligation of States under the Charter of the United Nations to promote universal respect for, and observance of, human rights and freedoms,

Realizing that the individual, having duties to other individuals and to the community to which he belongs, is under a responsibility to strive for the promotion and observance of the rights recognized in the present Covenant,

Agree upon the following articles:

[There follow 53, often multi-part, articles, which include the following rights:]

   Article 2: no discrimination based on race, colour, sex, language, religion, political, or other opinion, national or social origin, property, birth, or other status

Article 3: no sex discrimination

Article 5: no destruction of freedoms

Article 6: right to life

Article 7: no torture or cruel, inhuman or degrading treatment or punishment

Article 8: no slavery

Article 9: no arbitrary detention

Article 10: dignity of prisoners

Article 11: no prison for breach of contract

Article 12: right of movement

Article 13: no expulsion except pursuant to lawful decision

Article 14: equality before courts

Article 15: no punishment for retrospective offence

Article 16: recognition as person

Article 17: privacy

Article 18: freedom of thought

Article 19: freedom of opinion

Article 21: right of assembly

Article 22: freedom of association

Article 23: protection of family

Article 24: protection of children

Article 25: right to participate in the conduct of public affairs

Article 26: equality before the law

Article 27: as members of ethnic, religious or linguistic minorities, to enjoy their their own culture, to profess and practise their own religion, or to use their own language.

3. RIGHTS RECOGNISED BY VICTORIAN CHARTER OF HUMAN RIGHTS AND RESPONSIBILITIES

The Victorian Charter of Human Rights and Responsibilities Act 2006 (the Charter) came into full effect on 1 January 2008. It obliges all public authorities 'to give proper consideration to human rights in their decision-making and to act compatibly with the rights contained in the Charter when providing services and making decisions'.

The charter lists and details the following human rights that come with its ambit:

Section 8   Recognition and equality before the law

Section 9   Right to life

Section 10   Protection from torture and cruel, inhuman or degrading treatment

Section 11   Freedom from forced work

Section 12   Freedom of movement

Section 13   Privacy and reputation

Section 14   Freedom of thought, conscience, religion and belief

Section 15   Freedom of expression

Section 16   Peaceful assembly and freedom of association

Section 17   Protection of families and children

Section 18   Taking part in public life

Section 19   Cultural rights

Section 20   Property rights

Section 21   Right to liberty and security of person

Section 22   Humane treatment when deprived of liberty

Section 23   Children in the criminal process

Section 24   Fair hearing

Section 25   Rights in criminal proceedings

Section 26   Right not to be tried or punished more than once

Section 27   Retrospective criminal laws

(Equivalent rights are recognised by the ACT Human Rights Act.)

4. THE US BILL OF RIGHTS

The Conventions of a number of the States having, at the time of adopting the Constitution, expressed a desire, in order to prevent misconstruction or abuse of its powers, that further declaratory and restrictive clauses should be added, and as extending the ground of public confidence in the Government will best insure the beneficent ends of its institution;

Resolved, by the Senate and House of Representatives of the United States of America, in Congress assembled, two-thirds of both Houses concurring, that the following articles be proposed to the Legislatures of the several States, as amendments to the Constitution of the United States; all or any of which articles, when ratified by three-fourths of the said Legislatures, to be valid to all intents and purposes as part of the said Constitution, namely:

Amendment I
Congress shall make no law respecting an establishment of religion, or prohibiting the free exercise thereof; or abridging the freedom of speech, or of the press; or the right of the people peaceably to assemble, and to petition the government for a redress of grievances.

Amendment II
A well regulated militia, being necessary to the security of a free state, the right of the people to keep and bear arms, shall not be infringed.

Amendment III
No soldier shall, in time of peace be quartered in any house, without the consent of the owner, nor in time of war, but in a manner to be prescribed by law.

Amendment IV

The right of the people to be secure in their persons, houses, papers, and effects, against unreasonable searches and seizures, shall not be violated, and no warrants shall issue, but upon probable cause, supported by oath or affirmation, and particularly describing the place to be searched, and the persons or things to be seized.

Amendment V

No person shall be held to answer for a capital, or otherwise infamous crime, unless on a presentment or indictment of a grand jury, except in cases arising in the land or naval forces, or in the militia, when in actual service in time of war or public danger; nor shall any person be subject for the same offense to be twice put in jeopardy of life or limb; nor shall be compelled in any criminal case to be a witness against himself, nor be deprived of life, liberty, or property, without due process of law; nor shall private property be taken for public use, without just compensation.

Amendment VI

In all criminal prosecutions, the accused shall enjoy the right to a speedy and public trial, by an impartial jury of the state and district wherein the crime shall have been committed, which district shall have been previously ascertained by law, and to be informed of the nature and cause of the accusation; to be confronted with the witnesses against him; to have compulsory process for obtaining witnesses in his favor, and to have the assistance of counsel for his defense.

Amendment VII

In suits at common law, where the value in controversy shall exceed twenty dollars, the right of trial by jury shall be preserved, and no fact tried by a jury, shall be otherwise reexamined in any court of the United States, than according to the rules of the common law.

Amendment VIII

Excessive bail shall not be required, nor excessive fines imposed, nor cruel and unusual punishments inflicted.

Amendment IX

The enumeration in the Constitution, of certain rights, shall not be construed to deny or disparage others retained by the people.

Amendment X

The powers not delegated to the United States by the Constitution, nor prohibited by it to the states, are reserved to the states respectively, or to the people.

5. HUMAN-RIGHTS PROTECTION IN OTHER COUNTRIES

The United States

The provisions of the US Bill of Rights are set out in Appendix 4. Some parts of the Bill of Rights are famous (or infamous) and are widely known. They provide for:

1. Freedom of religion, speech, press, assembly, petition
2. The right to bear arms
3. No quartering of troops without consent
4. Restriction on search and seizure
5. Grand Jury, no double jeopardy, no self-incrimination, the right to due process
6. Criminal prosecutions — jury trial, right to confront accuser, right to counsel
7. Common law suits — jury trial
8. No excess bail or fines, cruel and unusual punishment
9. Non-enumerated rights
10. Rights reserved to states

The 11th Amendment abolished slavery. It was introduced directly after the end of the Civil War. The 13th Amendment made emancipation of slaves in America universal and permanent.

Supporting legislation

The rights set out in the Constitution are supported by Acts of Congress. They include, for example, the Civil Rights Acts of 1957, 1960, 1964, and 1968, which are enforced by the Civil Rights division of the Justice department; the Voting Rights Act of 1965, as amended through 1992; the Equal Credit Opportunity Act; the Americans with Disabilities Act; the National Voter Registration Act; the Uniformed and Overseas Citizens Absentee Voting Act; the Voting Accessibility for the Elderly and Handicapped Act; and additional civil-rights provisions contained in other laws and regulations. These laws prohibit discrimination in education, employment, credit, housing, public accommodations and facilities, voting, and certain federally funded and conducted programs.

State constitutions, statutes, and municipal ordinances provide further protection of civil rights.

Strength of protection

Because the Constitution is the supreme law of the land and the Bill of Rights is imposed upon the legislature 'by the people', the rights stated in it are guaranteed. If a piece of legislation goes against the Constitution it can be rendered invalid. However, the supporting Acts of Congress are more easily subject to change. Both private and public sectors are required to comply with the Constitution as well as the legislation.

Other organisations have their own arms that deal with specific civil-rights issues: for example, the Department of Health and Human Services has an Office for Civil Rights. They enforce a statutorily created civil right which states that 'all persons in the United States have a right to receive services in a non-discriminatory manner from state and local social and health services agencies, hospitals, clinics, nursing homes or other agencies receiving funds from HHS'.

All bodies dealing with civil-rights complaints encourage people to lodge their complaints within 180 days of the alleged offence. If good reason can be shown, the period may be extended.

When rights are breached

If someone believes one or more of their civil rights have been breached, their first point of contact is with one of the following bodies:

1. The Commission on Civil Rights (the commission) — primarily a referral body that puts people in contact with the appropriate federal, state, and local governments or private organisations who will further deal with the complaint. It lacks the power to enforce remedies; however, the commission can hold hearings through mediation processes and make recommendations. The commission also submits reports, findings, and recommendations to the president and Congress, and maintains state advisory committees. The majority of complaints involve discrimination based on race, colour, religion, sex, age, disability, or national origin.

2. The Department of Justice Civil Rights Division — this body operates within the federal government and is responsible for enforcing federal statutes prohibiting discrimination. Its power is restricted to government operations and federal matters.

If a civil-rights complaint requires legal investigation, the commission refers the matter, like any other legal proceedings, to the district court. The judiciary, most notably the Supreme Court, plays a crucial role in interpreting the extent of the civil rights. A single Supreme Court ruling can change the very nature of a right throughout the entire country. Supreme Court decisions can also affect the manner in which Congress enacts civil-rights legislation, as occurred with the Civil Rights Act of 1964. The federal courts were/are crucial in mandating and supervising school desegregation programs and other programs established to rectify state or local discrimination.

Canada

The primary document

The Canadian Charter of Rights and Freedoms is the primary source of human-rights protection in Canada. It is entrenched in the *Constitution Act 1982* and protects the following rights:

1. The rights and freedoms set out in it are guaranteed subject to reasonable limits prescribed by law
2. Fundamental freedoms: *a)* Freedom of conscience and religion; *b)* Freedom of thought, belief, opinion, and expression, including freedom of the press and other media of communication; *c)* Freedom of peaceful assembly; and *d)* Freedom of association.
3. The right to vote in an election.
4. Every citizen of Canada has the right to enter, remain and leave Canada.
5. The right to life, liberty, and security of person.
6. Security against unreasonable search and seizure.
7. The right not to be arbitrarily detained or imprisoned.
8. Upon arrest or detention, everyone has the right to: *a)* to be informed promptly of the reasons therefore; *b)* to retain and instruct counsel without delay and to be informed of that right; and *c)* to have the validity of the detention determined by way of *habeas corpus* and to be released if the detention is not lawful.
9. Any person charged with an offence has the right to:

a)   to be informed without unreasonable delay of the specific offence;

b)   to be tried within a reasonable time;

c)   not to be compelled to be a witness in proceedings against that person in respect of the offence;

d)   to be presumed innocent until proven guilty according to law in a fair and public hearing by an independent and impartial tribunal;

e)   not to be denied reasonable bail without just cause;

f)   except in the case of an offence under military law tried before a military tribunal, to the benefit of trial by jury where the maximum punishment for the offence is imprisonment for five years or a more severe punishment;

g)   not to be found guilty on account of any act or omission unless, at the time of the act or omission, it constituted an offence under Canadian or international law or was criminal according to the general principles of law recognised by the community of nations;

h)   if finally acquitted of the offence, not to be tried for it again and, if finally found guilty and punished for the offence, not to be tried or punished for it again; and

i)   if found guilty of the offence and if the punishment for the offence has been varied between the time of commission and the time of sentencing, to the benefit of the lesser punishment.

10. The right not to be subject to cruel and unusual punishment.

11. Equality before and under the law and cannot be subject to discrimination.

12. Equality of status between the languages of English and French.

13. The right to primary and secondary school education.

14. The right to apply to a court and seek remedy if a person

believes one or more of their rights set out in this Charter have been violated.

15. The freedoms in the Charter apply equally to males and females.

Supporting legislation

The *Canadian Human Rights Act 1977* (CHRA) is the other major protector of human rights. It is mainly concerned with discrimination, and applies largely to areas of employment, accommodation and commercial premises, including the private sector. It prohibits discrimination on the following grounds:

> Race, national or ethnic origin, colour, religion, age, sex, marital status, family status, sexual orientation, disability and conviction for which a pardon has been granted.

Strength of protection

The Charter is not subject to change because although it is in an act, it has been imposed by a superior legislature; it is an enactment of the United Kingdom parliament. The rights set out in the Charter are also protected, in that Section 52 states explicitly that 'the Constitution is the supreme law of Canada and any law that is inconsistent with the provisions of the Constitution is, to the extent of the inconsistency, of no force or effect'. Therefore, a piece of legislation or law that is inconsistent with the Charter may be rendered invalid by a court.

When rights are breached

If someone believes one or more of their civil rights have been breached, their first point of contact is with:

1. The Canadian Human Rights Commission. This organisation primarily deals with the administering of the

CHRA; however, any human-rights complaint is taken to the commission, which will deal with the problem, usually through mediation. If the complaint warrants further inquiry and/or an agreement can't be reached, they refer the case to the tribunal.

2. The Canadian Human Rights Tribunal (also operates as the Employment Equity Review Tribunal as stipulated in the *Employment Equity Act 1996*). The tribunal acts like a court and must therefore remain impartial. If a party wants a review of the tribunal's decision, they may be granted leave to appeal to the Federal Court of Canada.

New Zealand

The primary document

The New Zealand Bill of Rights Act 1990 is the primary source of human-rights legislation in New Zealand. It is dedicated to protecting human rights in general accordance with international declarations, namely the International Covenant on Civil and Political Rights (ICCPR) and the International Covenant on Economic, Social & Cultural Rights (ICESCR). The rights set out in the Bill of Rights Act are:

1. Right not to be deprived of life.
2. Right not to be subjected to torture or cruel treatment.
3. Right not to be subjected to medical or scientific experimentation.
4. Right to refuse to undergo medical treatment.
5. Electoral rights.
6. Freedom of thought, conscience, and religion.
7. Freedom of expression.
8. Manifestation of religion and belief.
9. Freedom of peaceful assembly.

10. Freedom of association.
11. Freedom of movement.
12. Freedom from discrimination.
13. Rights of minorities.
14. Unreasonable search and seizure.
15. Liberty of the person.
16. Rights of persons arrested or detained.
17. Rights of persons charged.
18. Minimum standards of criminal procedure.
19. Retroactive penalties and double jeopardy.
20. Right to justice.

Supporting legislation

The Human Rights Act 1993 (amended 2001) also exists. The Human Rights Act is principally concerned with discrimination. The relationship between the two acts has been problematic, especially regarding which Act should be used to set the standard for governmental activities — the standard set out in the Human Rights Act being at times impractical. The standard is now compared to section 19 of the Bill of Rights Act, which doesn't contain the detailed prescriptions of The Human Rights Act.

Strength of protection

The Bill of Rights Act is like any other act of the New Zealand parliament. It is not superior to any other legislation. In fact, section 4 states that inconsistent legislation, even if passed before the Bill of Rights, is not to be taken as impliedly repealed by the Bill of Rights, which could be interpreted as relegating the *Bill of Rights* to a status inferior to other enactments.

Treaties and conventions are binding on New Zealand courts when ratified and legislated into domestic statutes, but they may also be persuasive as a matter of statutory interpretation even when not ratified: in construing a piece of legislation in the event of ambiguity, the court will deem that parliament would not have chosen to legislate contrary to the spirit of an international treaty.

When rights are breached

If someone believes one or more of their rights have been breached, their first contact is with:

1. The Human Rights Commission — a statutory body that administers the Human Rights Act; however, it also deals with other human-rights complaints. It was established by the Human Rights Commission Act 1977. Under the Human Rights Act, this body is authorised to protect such rights in accordance with the United Nations Covenants and Conventions. The commission has the power to engage in dispute resolution; however, if no resolution can be reached, the matter is referred to the Human Rights Review Tribunal, which has the authority to enforce remedies. (The financial maximum the tribunal can impose is $200,000, the same as the district court).

2. The Human Rights Review Tribunal — Orders and decisions of the Human Rights Tribunal may be appealed to the High Court, and with the leave of the High Court to the Court of Appeal on questions of law.

3. Office of Human Rights Proceedings — established by the Human Rights Amendment Act 2001. The office's function is to provide, pursuant to statutory criteria, legal representation to people who have complained of alleged breaches of the Human Rights Act so that their claim can be litigated.

The United Kingdom
The primary document

The primary source of human-rights regulation is the *Human Rights Act 1998*, which came into force in October 2000. This act incorporates the rights specified in the European Convention for the Protection of Human Rights and Fundamental Freedoms (European Convention), which England ratified years ago. Prior to the Human Rights Act 1998, human-rights disputes had to be taken to the European Court of Human Rights, located in Strasbourg, which made such events costly. The rights protected are:

1. Obligation to respect human rights.
2. Right to life.
3. Prohibition of Torture.
4. Prohibition of slavery and forced labour.
5. Right to liberty and security.
6. Right to a fair trial.
7. No punishment without law.
8. Right to respect of private and family life.
9. Freedom of thought, conscience and religion.
10. Freedom of expression.
11. Freedom of assembly and association.
12. Right to marry.
13. Right to an effective remedy (when a right in this convention has been violated).
14. Prohibition of discrimination.
15. Derogation in time of emergency.
16. Restrictions on political activity of aliens.
17. Prohibition of abuse of rights.
18. Limitation on use of restrictions of rights.

Strength of protection
Section 3 of the Act states that the *Human Rights Act 1998* does not

have the status to render any other legislation invalid should an issue of incompatibility arise. There have been 10 incompatibility complaints in three years. However, there is still the opportunity for someone in England to take their complaint to the European Court of Human Rights if they believe a Convention right has been breached, so in that respect the level of protection is two-tiered.

When rights have been breached

If someone believes one or more of their rights have been breached, they should seek legal advice. The procedure for dealing with human-rights violations is the same as if making any other legal complaint (civil). At this point in time, there are no human-rights commissions that can deal with matters through alternative processes such as mediation. A proposal to set up a commission for equality and human rights was made in late 2003; however, nothing is in place yet. Generally, complaints must be brought within a year of the alleged offence taking place.

6. EXTRACTS FROM THE REPORT OF THE AUSTRALIAN SENATE'S LEGAL AND CONSTITUTIONAL REFERENCES COMMITTEE ON LEGAL AID AND ACCESS TO JUSTICE (JUNE 2004)

Paragraph 2.88 The Committee is concerned that the Commonwealth Priorities and Guidelines deny adequate assistance in family and civil matters.

Paragraph 4.22 Evidence presented to the Committee suggests that there is gender disparity in the distribution of Legal Aid funds in practice, resulting in indirect but significant discrimination against the circumstances and needs of women in their access to justice. The

Committee is concerned about the Commonwealth Government's apparent lack of recognition of some of the particularly grave consequences of family law disputes. The Committee does not believe that Legal Aid funding for criminal law matters should come at the expense of funding for family law.

Paragraph 4.49 The Committee agrees that the 'cap' in relation to family law funding creates significant problems. The Committee believes that if the 'cap' is to remain, there needs to be greater discretion to exceed it in particular cases. However, the Committee reiterates its view in the Third Report that, given the lack of funding generally, 'any exercise of the discretion becomes an exercise in robbing Peter to pay Paul.' It is not appropriate that applicants in more expensive cases benefit at the expense of other equally meritorious applicants. The Committee strongly believes that more funding is required.

Paragraph 4.70 The Committee considers that it is imperative that there be adequate funding of legal assistance for actions taken under state/territory law involving domestic violence since the scope for action under Commonwealth law is extremely limited.

Paragraph 4.100 The Committee shares the concerns of a number of witnesses in relation to the high levels of self-representing women in family law matters. In particular, the Committee considers that where violence has taken place, legal representation is needed to ensure that women can participate effectively in the legal system.

Paragraph 5.123 The Committee is gravely concerned by the evidence it received about the overwhelming deficiencies in the Legal Aid system as it relates to Indigenous people in Australia, particularly those living in remote areas.

Paragraph 6.80 Evidence presented to the Committee during the course of the inquiry clearly indicates that gaps in the Legal Aid system are greatly magnified in RRR areas. Overwhelmingly, the evidence suggests that the current arrangements throughout RRR areas of Australia are inconsistent and inadequate ...

Paragraph 7.26 The Committee is concerned that the Guidelines introduced in 1997 have resulted in a reduction of available legal assistance for migrants and refugees ...

Paragraph 7.27 Migrants and refugees are amongst the most disadvantaged groups in terms of access to justice.

Paragraph 8.21 The Committee considers that improving access to justice is essential to breaking the cycle that leads to homelessness and poverty ...

Paragraph 9.40 The Committee considers pro bono legal services to be an important and growing part of the response to the need for legal assistance. However, it is neither a substitute for an adequately funded Legal Aid system nor a panacea for overcoming gaps in other publicly funded legal services ...

Paragraph 10.42 The Committee is disappointed that the Government continues to avoid collecting empirical data on a fundamental issue in the Legal Aid funding debate: whether the costs saved by reducing Legal Aid funding are outweighed by the costs potentially caused by an increasing number of self-represented litigants ...

Paragraph 10.95 There is much evidence to demonstrate a strong link between restrictions on Legal Aid funding and the growing numbers of self-represented litigants. The Committee is concerned about this increase and the impact it may have on the administration of justice ...

Paragraph 11.46 The Committee strongly believes that CLCs have a vital role to play in helping to achieve a fairer and more effective Legal Aid system that is available and accessible to all Australians. It is important that CLCs are properly funded to enable them to provide services that can be responsive to community need. The Committee considers the difficulties CLCs are experiencing to be unacceptable. These difficulties appear to be a direct result of inadequate levels of funding and increased demand on CLCs, caused by restricted LAC funding.